THE FORTY YEAR OLD MOVIE VIRGIN

Mike Oughton

THE FORTY YEAR OLD MOVIE VIRGIN

An ad man makes
a feature film.

Cover Photograph by John Martin

All other photographs © Mike Oughton

Cover design by Gary Todd

ISBN: 9781521559222

To Patsy.

For everything you are and everything you do.

About The Forty-Year-Old Movie Virgin

Mike Oughton is an Advertising Copywriter and Creative Director with over twenty years of experience.

As an antidote to a day job spent flogging people stuff they don't necessarily want, he devotes his spare time to writing feature films. And books about the making of them.

He lives in Greenwich, London.

PART ONE

PRE-PRODUCTION

FIRST POST

THIS IS THE FIRST SENTENCE of my first book, which is about my first feature film. Well, it's not the first film I've written - it's the second - but it is the first film I've written, in collaboration with my director mate, that has actually amounted to more than just a sheaf of paper for people to read. In exactly one week it will be Day One of my first feature film shoot. My mate's directing. The cast is all cast. And I'm wetting myself with excitement. Figuratively, but only just.

It's seven days until we start filming and it's six months since we signed the option agreement with our ninja-esque producers. It's also one year and eight months since my director mate and I shot an excerpt of the feature-length story as a short film to attract funding. And I've just checked my files and, incredibly, it is exactly four years to the day since I saved the first document of this project in my 'Secret Projects' folder on my work computer. It's taken precisely four years and twenty-eight drafts, written in the spare time I've had whilst holding down a demanding job in advertising. I have sacrificed countless weekends, burned mucho holiday entitlement and tested the loyalty and patience of my better half, far more than she has deserved. But today I got to a point I never really believed I'd ever get to. Today my final script was officially 'locked down' for production. The next few months are going to be a mad adventure for a middle-aged man. My family and friends are excited for me. So, on the suggestion of my mate, Lee, I've decided to write it all down as it happens, both as an aide memoir in the future and a way of excusing myself from having to phone everyone the whole time to let them know what's going on.

I know it's a Monday. I know I have an important meeting with a recently won new client in the morning, but sod-it, I'm opening a bottle of something.

RECONNAISSANCE

MY DIRECTOR MATE is on the 'tech recce' today. Sorry, I'm going to have to try and stop using jargon here as not everyone will have a didgeridoo what I'm on about. Sorry, there I go again: didgeridoo = clue. Anyway, the technical recce is the part in the process when the film crew visit all the locations in the film, to work out what camera positions and angles they will be filming. And what equipment they will need to achieve it (lenses, lights, types of camera rig, blah blah). My director mate keeps sending me photos of various places in London - the film's set in London, by the way - with lots of excited exclamation-mark-filled text accompanying them. In each photograph the sky is bright blue and the light is perfect.

I'm elated and gutted all at once. That's because, while all this exciting gallivanting around London is going on, I'm at work writing ads for a leading condiment brand, and a new client who represent a leading chocolate bar brand.

Oh well, before I get the violins out I read an email from an old workmate who quit advertising eleven years ago on the back of a screenplay he'd sold to Hollywood. He was a big inspiration to me to pick up my quill, and I had emailed him to thank him for his encouragement down the years. In his reply he said that his film had gone through five directors and three production companies and STILL hadn't been made yet. It is a sobering fact that explains why I can't effin believe this is actually happening to me.

ME AND THE DIRECTOR

THE DIRECTOR AND I are both from the advertising industry. I'm a creative director in an advertising agency. I write commercials, posters, press ads etc. and I also manage other people, 'creative directing' their work on behalf of the clients that I am responsible for.

My mate is a commercials director. He started off writing the ads, like I do, in an ad agency, but became a director about twenty years ago. He is multi-award winning and co-owns a commercials production company.

It's funny, because even though making this film is a hugely exciting new adventure for us both, we are actually seasoned filmmakers in our own way. I'm a writer and maker of thirty-second films for about nineteen years. He's the director of four-hundred-plus commercials. So we know our way around a page of dialogue and a film set, all right. It's just that, to the film industry, having experience in the commercial filmmaking world means absolutely eff-all.

We met about fifteen years ago. Jesus, time flies. Our golden arch of a writer-director relationship began when I hired him to direct a commercial I'd written for a well-known global fast food chain. Somehow, I had convinced the client that the best way to promote their new Indian burger was to remake one of those old 1970s Pearl and Dean cinema ads you used to get for the local curry house 'just minutes from this cinema'.

The director and I really got on well during the production. We come from fairly similar backgrounds and have similar creative sensibilities. (Basically, we both like taking the piss.) The fact that the commercial won loads of ad awards didn't hurt, either. So I worked with him several times more. Once for the same well-known restaurant chain, promoting their new Jungle Burger, which meant two weeks in Puerto effin Rico, thank you very much.

After a few years of working together, my director mate started talking about his desire to get into feature films. I was a little taken aback when he suggested we team up and write a screenplay together. I'd never written anything longer than sixty seconds before and certainly had no pretension - or the tiniest germ of a concept in my head, even - that writing a film is something I could do. But seeing as this top ad director who had his pick of advertising writers in London, had chosen to approach me, I was bewilderingly flattered into giving it a pop.

I then proceeded to pretty much waste half the spare time of my thirties chipping away at a couple of feature film projects with him. Until, as I neared the four-oh mark, we actually got a production deal. And it suddenly wasn't 'wasted time' and more, it was 'an investment that paid off'. Phew!

PPM

I SOMEHOW MANAGED TO SNEAK OUT of the office for the morning today, in order to attend the pre-production meeting. This is the final meeting before the shoot, where all aspects of the production are officially agreed.

We have them in advertising. I find them to be loathsome excruciating pedantry-fests, as a rule. But not this one. That's because, unlike in advertising, there was no client. So we didn't have to spend an inordinate amount of effort sourcing several options and constructing convincing arguments regarding the merits of everything from the script, cast, locations, music, props, or the colour of the jumper the actor will be wearing.

Oh yeah, anyone in advertising who says they haven't spent three quarters of an hour arguing with a client about jumper colour is a wretched two-faced liar. (Not necessarily bad qualities to possess for a successful advertising career.)

Yes, even though twenty-eight people attended the meeting to discuss a production approximately one hundred and eighty times longer than the average thirty-second commercial, it was a remarkably pain-free experience. I would even go as far as to say that I enjoy being part of a meeting full of talented experts from all film departments (camera, electrical, production, art, wardrobe, make-up, editing) all pulling in the same direction to make the production come together.

I return to work with a shit-eating grin that surprises and irritates my colleagues in equal measure. I explain that the reason for this almost unprecedented me-smiling-at-work occurrence was the equally unprecedented enjoyable Pre-production meeting. And one of them replies: "Of course you enjoyed it. You're the client". Smile wiped.

LAST DAY AT WORK

THIS FILM IS SUCH BIG DEAL to me, I am fully prepared to hand my notice in at work if they don't allow me to take the time off to attend the shoot.

It sounds drastic. I may well be paranoid, but the fact is, advertising is a harsh and fickle industry when it wants to be. It is performance based and highly competitive. The creative side of the business that I do - coming up with ideas and making ads - is very subjective. Agencies are constantly looking for fresh, exciting approaches to creative work. So having a 'churn' of creative people is common.

You could work in a place for five-plus years and be very well liked and respected, but all it takes is a new boss to come in who doesn't like the cut of your jib, and before you know it, you're out on your ear.

It's tricky, because UK employment law doesn't take 'face fitting' into account, so advertising is renowned for paying people off to get rid of them. It's happened to loads of my colleagues down the years. It even happened to me once, when my creative team partner and myself* were fired because our boss thought my art director was 'a middle-class rugger bugger twat'. I'm not an expert, but I don't think that constitutes particularly reasonable grounds for dismissal, really. Never mind, we got a job somewhere better straight away and I was able to buy a new car with the payoff. (The art director bought himself a flash motorbike.)

Anyway, my current bosses have only been at this agency for eight months, so I'm still not completely sure if my face fits with them or not. Having a creative sideline - a really cool one - could easily put a creative boss' nose out of joint**, or make them think I'm not committed to the job. That's why the first time they knew I'd written a feature film was the morning, three weeks ago, when I asked them for a sabbatical. I didn't want them to think that I'm anything less than one hundred percent committed to their cause.

Thankfully, the resignation letter remains unwritten, as they are okay with it. In fact, they seem genuinely impressed and happy for me, which is nice. Sabbaticals are discretionary at my agency, so being granted six weeks off is very generous of them. It also serves as a face-fit affirmation.

Great. All things being equal, I would like to stay. I am enjoying it more since their arrival (and the film stuff kicking off). A month ago I won a new chocolate bar advertising account for the agency. It was won after a protracted three-month pitch process that wiped out whole swathes of my evenings and weekends. I am currently writing television commercial scripts for the brand. And luckily, they will be researched with consumers while I'm away from work filming my movie, so I might not miss too much.

Yes, I love my day job. Wanting to stay employed and not take the leap into full-time screenwriting is all to do with the creative nourishment advertising gives me and nothing to do with the humongous mortgage hanging around my neck like a fucking lead weight. Honest.

As I leave the agency for the last time for six weeks with a skip in my step, I am dying to bid farewell to my colleagues with a jaunty: 'See ya later, losers!'

I don't, though. Not because I'm nice, but because it's half past nine at night and everyone else has gone home. These chocolate bar ads don't write themselves, you know.

* *In advertising, we work in 'creative teams' of two, traditionally made up of a copywriter and an art director. Words and pictures. Basically, it's two people sitting in an office coming up with ideas. Only, in the execution of said ideas, one is responsible for the writing and the other, the visual side. A good creative team is better than the sum of their parts and can spend their whole careers together, moving from agency to agency, as a team. It's like a marriage.*

However, this working model is being challenged. The rise of technology means code writers are also now part of creative departments, so they can create exciting and imaginative apps for brands that people never use.

** *The only other bloke in advertising I know who sold a feature film script (the one I was telling you about who still hasn't had it produced) got kicked out of the agency he worked at when his boss found out. I can only imagine his boss was a budding screenwriter, too, and resented his charge's achievement.*

PART TWO
PRODUCTION

DAY 1. SCENE 1. TAKE 1

I'm sitting on set, next to my director mate. We're ten minutes from 'turning over' (filming). The very first scene we're shooting is the opening shot of the film. This is a really rare occurrence. Even when making a commercial you rarely, if ever, shoot sequentially. However, the sequential filming lasts for only one scene. There are babies in the film. And due to strict child-labour laws, the whole production schedule has been planned around the little sods.

This afternoon we're doing a really important and dramatic scene from much later in the story. It's a scene that the director and I did a little re-think on over the weekend. (Because we can. Mwa ha ha ha!). Nothing major, but it meant new dialogue and a couple of new props. It took me fifteen minutes on Sunday to write. But a further four hours to format it correctly. This is because once you've got a 'locked' movie script, any changes you make thereafter have to be specifically annotated. Each crew member has a hard copy of the script, you see, which they have, no doubt, marked with their own notes. So re-issuing a whole new script every time there is a change is impractical and confusing.

Instead, just the individual changed pages are issued on different coloured paper in a way that doesn't alter the page and scene numbers of the subsequent scenes, so people can physically replace them in their hard copies. It sounds complicated, and it is. I've been using the Final Draft screenwriting package for years, but I had to give myself a crash course tutorial in how to revise a production script.

My head hurts by the end of it. As a result, I treat myself to Shiraz, reasoning that it will help me sleep ahead of the big first day. It doesn't.

PR DISASTER

THE SUN IS OUT TODAY. It gives the most glorious clear views across London from the fourteenth floor apartment we're filming in. Nightmare. It was snowing a bloody blizzard yesterday. (It's the middle of March, FFS!) As anyone who has ever been on a film set knows, these extremes of weather are really bad for continuity. Even a short scene in a movie can take several hours or days to be shot. So if it's bright sunshine one day, but blizzard conditions the next, it can really ruin something that's supposed to feel like continuous action in a film.

During a break in filming to let the blizzard conditions pass, I have a Twitter conversation with my mate from Manchester where I explain this very point. I literally think nothing more of said conversation - I only have about fifty Twitter followers, he has less - until late last night when my director mate forwards me an internet link accompanied by the words: *'U r classy....'.*

I click on the link, and to my delight, it's an article about the film in the online version of a famous national magazine. As well as our brilliant leading actors, my director mate and myself are also name-checked. This is big time. Get in! However, my elation lasts precisely one sentence until I read: *'It's effin freezing down here'* *the writer tweeted earlier today from the film set 'It's snowing! Gonna right f***k up our continuity!'*

Yes, I am, indeed, a classy guy.

35MM, 2-PERF*

WE ARE SHOOTING this movie on 35mm film. It's the first time in years that either myself, or the director have filmed on actual film. Most commercials, and an increasing number of movies, are shot on digital cameras these days. Digital is amazing. We shot our short film on a digital SLR camera bought on the high street, and it looked the nuts.

It somehow feels 'proper' that we're using real film stock for this. It does to me, anyway. And it means that those old-fashioned film-set phrases can be heard, like: 'Check the gate!' 'There's a hair in the gate!' 'There's another hair in the gate!' and 'Bloody hell, this set is hairier than a barbershop floor!'**.

It's more expensive to shoot this way, so it makes you think harder and longer about shots than you would with digital. Take this morning, for example. It's the scene where our brilliant lead actress uses the kitchen sink. We are just about to 'turn over' when the director suddenly gets anxious about the fact that there is a toaster sat next to the sink. After a quick discussion, we reassure ourselves that this is not a commercial. We are not going to get in trouble with Clearcast (the advertising compliance body) for this potentially dangerous positioning of electrical equipment in shot.

So, while all the crewmembers without an advertising background look at us like we're mental, we edge the toaster even more dangerously close to the sink. Why? We're in the movies now, baby, and that's how we roll. So roll film, and... Action!

A 35mm film magazine, yesterday.

** 35mm refers to the width of the film passing through the camera.'2-perf' refers to height of each frame, by numbering the amount of perforations that run along the side of each frame of the film on the roll.*

Conventional film has four perforations per frame. However, shooting a movie in a cinematic letterbox format using '4-perf' only uses half of the depth of the frame. Therefore, it allows filmmakers to adjust the framing in the edit, should they wish, by 'racking' up or down. '3-perf' allows a little bit of reframing and is cheaper than

'4-perf', because it means you can fit more frames on each roll of film. '2-perf' film is cheaper still, but as each frame of film is the same shape as the letterbox format, there is no room for reframing, whatsoever. (Unless you zoom in on the image, that is, but doing that more than about 10% loses too much picture definition.)

*** After every scene, the inside of a film camera is checked for foreign bodies. Not actual hairs, but usually tiny hairline shavings that come off the roll of film as it passes through the camera. If there is a 'hair in the gate' it means the stuff you've just shot is probably unusable and you've got to go again. Especially if you're using 2-perf and you have no room to 'rack' your framing up or down in the edit suite****.*

**** Many thanks to the Director of Photography for the above information. I had assumed the clapper loader had alopecia. (The clapper loader is the person in charge of loading and unloading the film in the camera.)*

RUSHES

A NICE THING ABOUT SHOOTING on film is the daily rushes, or 'dailies'. Every day, selected takes from the footage shot the previous day are rushed back from the film-processing lab for us to watch. We check that, lighting-wise, each shot looks how intended. We see whether any of the 'hair in the gate' stuff is usable or not. And if the acting performances are as captivating as we thought they were on the day. We also get a report back from the editor, who is starting to select takes and build sequences, as to how it's working as a piece of storytelling and if we've missed anything.

You don't get rushes shooting on a digital camera, because it's instantaneous. Obviously, instantaneous is better, but it's not nearly as magical. Much the same as digital stills cameras are better, but have robbed us of that beautiful sense of anticipation and excitement we used to get when collecting our holiday prints from Boots or Snappy Snaps.

Jesus. I have just read that back and I remind me of my Nan explaining to the eight-year-old me why she liked the wireless more than the telly.

Sorry. It's deja vu all round today, as the latest rushes we receive are from the beginning of the story and, therefore, scenes we also shot eighteen months ago when we made the short film trailer. Seeing the same action reshot is a little weird. It's weird in a 'Shit the bed! I'm on a movie set and those actors are speaking my words!' kind of way.

Everyone is happy with the rushes, so far. Which is great news, as watching bad rushes is the movie equivalent of standing outside Snappy Snaps with your fading suntan, looking at photographs that the hotel cleaners took of themselves scrubbing the toilet bowl with your toothbrush.

ON-SET TANTRUMS

THE LAST COUPLE OF DAYS on set have been tense. We've been filming babies. They are difficult to film, are babies. You just can't reason with the little sods. If they want to look directly into the camera during a take, soil themselves at inopportune moments, or cry constantly for three hours, there's not a thing you can do about it. It's probably a bit like working with Marlon Brando in his later years. But I suppose at least with Marlon you didn't have the added nightmare of the ultra strict child labour laws that mean they are only allowed on set for four hours per day. We've got around it as far as we can by casting identical twins. But they are conditioned by their parents to eat and sleep at the same time, so if one is kicking off, invariably the other one is in the same state of mind.

The director and myself have tried our best to rewrite and simplify the script as much as possible to accommodate the wee treasures as much as possible. The scene where a precocious eleven-month-old baby plays a Mozart sonata faultlessly on piano is now 'We see a baby sitting in the middle of a room screaming for its mother then crawling out of frame'.

The director keeps cracking the same 'who wrote this bloody script?' joke in my presence. Glad everyone else finds it funny. I resolve never to work on a Pampers commercial and make a quick mental check that my other screenplay has no babies in it. It doesn't. It does have a dog licking its own balls, but all you need for that is a bit of strategically placed Marmite, apparently.

SUPERVISION

THE AVERAGE TV AD is thirty seconds long. If you're really lucky, a client may cough up for a sixty or ninety-second slot. And I've done a couple of online ads that nudged past the three-minute mark. But I've never been involved in anything as long and complicated as this ninety-five-minute story. Or a whopping one hundred and ninety commercials, back-to-back, if you want to send a shiver up the director's spine.

We know how long the story is because it was timed out by our Script Supervisor. We don't tend to have Script Supervisors in commercials very often, so it's been good to meet and work with one over the last week. Like everyone, I've seen the job title on film credits. But I never really knew the depth of their involvement.

Pre-production, they time out and script edit the screenplay. Then, during production they are the point of reference between editor and director, logging all the technical stuff that I haven't got a clue about.

They are also in charge of all continuity during the shoot. Stuff like making sure a phone is in an actor's pocket, because it's going to ring three scenes later, the clock on the wall is telling the right time, or if an actor folds their arms a certain way in one take, they fold them in exactly the same way in all the subsequent shots so the scene can be edited seamlessly. Basically, all the shit that makes my head hurt.

If I were being unkind, I'd say it was a job for the most anal person in the world. But seeing as she's really nice, and said nice things about the tightness of the script, I'd say she is blessed with an incredible eye for detail, and I am in awe.

I liked her before I met her, actually, because when she timed the script at ninety-five minutes, it was a two-fingered salute to a lot of people who had read the script along the way and criticized it for being too short. (This doesn't include our producers, I hasten to add, who really know their onions.) The general rule of thumb is that a page of script is equal to a minute of screen time. However, it varies massively depending on how dialogue heavy it is. Ours is only about thirty percent dialogue, so is a lot shorter on the page than it will be on screen. Well, that's the plan, anyway. Fingers crossed and all that.

LATE CALL

SCRIPT WRITING is all about opportunity. Whether it's a feature film you're writing or a dog food commercial. You literally start with a blank piece of paper and your job is to fill it with the most compelling, imaginative, exciting stuff you can. Down the years I've had loads of amazing experiences thanks to the crap I've written down in a script.

I've written myself holidays in South Africa, France, Germany, The US, Brazil, Lesotho, Puerto Rico, Spain, Czech Republic, Finland, Ireland, Sweden, Slovakia, Canada, and probably several others I have forgotten.

However, if you can't write yourself a fabulous shoot somewhere exotic, write something that can be shot within walking distance of your house. That's what I say. This film is about a London ad executive*, so I've plumped for the latter rather than the former. Most days I have had the absolute pleasure of a thirty-five-minute stroll to the set. Except when it's been snowing or raining or I can't be arsed.

The walk is something I need to do to counteract the twenty-six days of sitting in front of a playback monitor, eating shoot food. Commercials are typically one to three day shoots. It's typically one to three days of filling your boots with full English breakfasts, big lunches with side salads and puddings. And if you have any room (I do), afternoon tea, cakes and sandwiches. When you shoot a commercial in LA, you also have 'craft services', which is basically a fat bloke walking around set all day handing out donuts and M&Ms.

I've had to have a serious word with myself to not hoover up all the free food that's knocking about. I've tapered my breakfast intake from full English, a few days of bacon sarnie, and now, just toast and fruit. And I've elbowed the puddings at lunchtime. I don't think I'll ever pass up a cheese and pickle triangle or six at teatime, though.

The food situation is further complicated by the schedule. We're shooting a lot of split days, so it's late starts and late finishes. We get 'brunch' from eleven am, lunch/dinner at five pm and the tray of sandwiches usually arrives around eight-ish, for an eleven pm wrap (finish). Having the mornings free is strangely liberating for an office worker, like myself. I planned to get up early every day and go for a run, but needless to say, the most I've done with my mornings is write these updates.

Right, the call-time is in forty-five minutes. Better get my skates on. Not literally.

**Don't worry. The film isn't about the ad industry.*

THREE HANDER

WE'VE BEEN SHOOTING my favourite scene for the last two nights. The scene features three people sitting around a table, eating a meal. It's dialogue heavy and complex. Each character has a completely different motivation and knowledge of the situation they are in. And there's loads of subtext flying about. I've acted it out in my head and fiddled with the dialogue more than an advertising art director with OCD fiddles with a layout. Despite this, I've lived in hope rather than expectation that it plays out as excruciatingly as intended. To shoot it, we've cut the scene in half. But each take is still five minutes long. This is a completely new experience for me. Proper filming!

We shoot with two cameras so we can capture close-ups as well as the master wide shots at the same time. This is very useful, because the reactions are as important as the dialogue.

The results are better than I hoped. Much better. Our actors are amazing. In the words of Simon Cowell, they've taken the lyrics and completely made them their own. I'm floating. The feeling you get when something you've written is brought to life so well is indescribable. So I won't. And I won't pretend this indescribable feeling doesn't also happen when making a commercial. I was positively dewy eyed when the hero of my last production nailed his performance. But great an actor as 'Man Dressed as Giant Turkey' was, this is a different ball game.

Lots of people in a small room, yesterday.

SEX SCENE

JESUS, I AM REALLY in unknown territory now. In my whole advertising career, I've never even filmed a kissing scene before, let alone a full on fuck fest. I say 'fest'. The scene we are filming tonight is more of a drunken bunk-up on a sofa, to be honest. In fact, it's not supposed to be romantic or erotic in any way. If anything, we want the audience to be revolted by it. But I don't know if that makes it any less embarrassing or difficult for the actors to perform. I say 'perform'. It's more of an awkward entanglement, really.

It's pretty effin embarrassing for me, that's for sure. Seriously, you sit down and write this stuff, but you don't think the consequences through properly. I've had to meet the actors, look them in the eye and discuss things with them like positions and states of nakedisation. (Made up word. Probably a real one in America.) The conversation is about how many clothes can be kept on rather than strewn. No mention of areolae or arse cheekery, whatsoever.

Missionary is the agreed position. The director demonstrates the action on the sofa for the benefit of the actors. I kick myself that I didn't video it on my phone. What an insight that was!

Despite my anxiety, the actors take it all in their stride and nail it like pros. I say 'pros'. I mean fine actors, not 'pros'.

VIOLENCE

ANOTHER DAY, ANOTHER BRILLIANT experience. Today we're indulging in a bit of the old ultra-violence, my droogs*. Cool. As. Hell. The director and I hail from an industry where you are not even allowed to show a person driving a car without a seatbelt. So being able to film our actors knocking seven shades of shit out of each other all day really makes our hearts sing.

We sit behind the monitor (the TV screen that plays what the camera sees) with boyish grins on our faces as right-hander after right-hander is thrown and nose splitting head butts cause enough claret to flow to rival any 'pwopa nawty' football hooligan movie. I clarify all this straight away by saying we're not making an action film. There are a couple of violent scenes in it, is all. Our cast is made up of highly accomplished performers, not plastic gangsters, I'll have you know. But I think they appreciate the novelty of indulging in a bit of physical stuff, nonetheless. Our stunt coordinator choreographs the scenes with them. (Oh yeah, we've got a stunt coordinator, baby.) Yet, even though not a single real blow is landed in anger, it's still a bloody demanding challenge. It looks pretty challenging from where I'm sitting sipping my cup of tea, anyway.

The actors rise to it. Humble and polite off set, our male lead is terrifying on screen. And our BLA (Brilliant Leading Actress) is as astonishingly mesmeric to watch as always, even with half a pint of fake blood pouring out of her hooter. Now that is talent.

It's all kicking off.

* *If you don't understand this reference, well shame on you.*

ART DEPARTMENT

I LIKE HANGING OUT with the art department. They are in charge of everything you see in front of the camera that isn't an actor. These are the set designers, the art directors and the prop makers. Even though ours is considered a small production - Lord Of The Rings, it ain't - there are loads of art dept. bods swarming about. It's fair enough, because they've got a lot on their plate.

Our primary location, for example, is a 'cool docklands apartment'. We've rented a docklands apartment, but the art department has had to work their magic to add the 'cool' bit. They've completely redecorated and refurnished the place, fitted a new kitchen and turned a bedroom closet into a functioning high-end bathroom.

Another thing the art department do is make sure we have permission to use every branded item that appears on screen. Everything we don't get permission to use, they have to design and build a look-a-likey version of. Right now, they are creating the exterior of a dive-in fast food restaurant. This is because a certain well-known fast food chain has a no-filming policy on their premises. The director and I are particularly indignant about this shun. We met fifteen years ago while making a commercial for that fast food joint. The drive-thru scene was our little homage to it, but the fucking fuckers have fucking well fucked it.

During the shoot, the art dept. team of eight to ten split themselves into two groups. Three are on set. These are the 'stand-by art directors'. It is their job to arrange each scene correctly, ensure continuity, and be on stand-by to shift the props around the set when and where needed. Meanwhile, the rest of the department, are in a windowless room somewhere designing and making all the props and sets. I've found them to be a passionate, talented bunch that take the visual aspects of the script and really run with them.

Good production design can add another layer to the feel and depth of the story that you'd never find in the script. The other day, the head production designer told me she'd deliberately chosen certain props in the film to be red, thereby attaching a symbolic thread of danger to a particular character. Great stuff. It's this sort of depth that fans of Stanley Kubrick films write theses and make web films about. (Seriously, have a look on YouTube.) And it's stuff that I will pretend was in the script from the beginning if anyone ever notices and comments upon*.

** Only joking. I would never pass off others' work as my own. The director would, but I wouldn't.*

GOING UNDERGROUND

TODAY WE'RE SPENDING the whole day in a basement car park. It's the car park of the tower block our apartment is in. Down in the bowels of the building, it may be out of the elements, but it is bloody freezing nonetheless. It's the end of March. I'm wearing a massive parker jacket, two more layers underneath, jeans and long johns. And I'm still absolutely freezing.

Something you learn very early on when being on film sets is to always wear more clothes than you imagine you need. It's alright if you're part of the actual crew - the art department, lighting department or camera department - and your job keeps you moving all day. (Lots of those guys wear shorts all year round.) However, if your job on set is involves merely sitting in front of a monitor, you need to layer up, baby.

Today is a particular case in point. I thought I'd be fine in trainers, seeing as we're inside in the dry. I was wrong. The cold seems to be seeping up through the concrete basement floor to chill me from the feet up. Damn. I've got some hardcore hiking boots that are good to temperatures of -50°C at home that would be really toasty right now*.

We're shooting two scenes down here today. They are both really important moments in the film. The first scene sees the main character pull a heavy item out of an elevator. She then leaves the item and sprints across the car park, jumps in her car and reverses, at speed, back to the heavy item so she can bundle it into the trunk of the car. All before the elevator returns to the basement with a possible witness.

It's quite an adrenal scene. And is quite tricky to shoot, because there are lots of elements to it.

The first tricky element is the fact that the actual elevator to the basement isn't in an appropriate place for our filming. Therefore, the art department has had to build one as a prop. The dummy lift doesn't have to go anywhere, and we will paint in the LED floor indicator thing as an effect in post-production, but the doors need to open and close convincingly. The art department nail it.

Our BLA (brilliant lead actress) wears a full-length quilted coat between takes, but just a thin trouser suit when we film. Mercifully, her action is all action, dragging the heavy item multiple times while we film from different angles.

Then she has to sprint the length of the car park to her car, loads of times. She runs with an impressively athletic gate. I remark on this fact to her between takes and she explains that she played Rugby League to a high standard as a teenager. Multi-talented. However, we do not test her driving skills for the high-speed car reversal in the scene, because we have a stunt driver.

I spend fully twenty minutes trying to get a photo on my phone of our main actress standing next to the identically attired stuntwoman (including a wig) who will be performing the precision driving.

She's great at it. Spinning the car out of its space and tanking it in reverse to stop with screeching breaks right on the mark every time. I mention to the director that it would be funny if the reversing car drives over the heavy item, instead. (Okay, I need to say here that the heavy item is, in fact, a dead body. So when I say 'funny' I actually mean 'really dark humoured'.)

The director thinks it's a great idea. We spend the best part of another three-quarters of an hour re-choreographing the scene to incorporate this script improvisation. The producers aren't happy, though, as it's forty-five minutes out of our day and we have got a lot to fit in.

On a commercial you constantly go over time on stuff. You end up paying the crew overtime. It's the way it goes. On this low budget movie set, there is no such luxury. Everyone in the cast and crew is on a deal which means nobody is going to get rich off this, so we can't take liberties with the length of the working day.

Besides, the film industry is probably the most unionized business operating in the UK. The film union is stronger than even the tube workers' union, I reckon. Hence, the strict adherence of breaks, provision of meals and refreshments, working hours and overtime rates. We simply cannot afford to pay any overtime on this production. However, we get to the end of the day and we still have one more really crucial scene to shoot. It is actually the climax of act one of the story, FFS!

I can practically hear the music from hit quiz show Countdown ringing in my ears as the director argues with the producer about how much time we've got on this last, really crucial scene. Oops. If we hadn't messed about with that extra shot, we'd be fine.

In the event, we literally get one take of this all-important shot. Thankfully, our BLA (brilliant leading actress) isn't called a BLA (brilliant leading actress) for nothing. She saves our flabby arses by nailing it in one.

Phew. That's a harsh lesson in the difference between commercials and movies learned right there.

* *I got the boots to wear when shooting a commercial for a well-known brand of vodka alcopop in the Tetris Mountains of Slovakia a few years back. It was -30°C. Even breathing hurt.*

My feet were toasty enough when I was walking around, but again, because my job on set was to sit/stand beside the monitor watching what was being filmed, the cold just seeped up through the pack ice I was standing on.

Not good, but to be fair to the manufacturer's claim, they are designed to be good to -50°C when hiking, not hanging about watching telly in a blizzard.

END OF AN ERA

THERE IS JOY tinged with a bit of sadness today. It's the last day of filming in our prime location on the Isle of Dogs. We've definitely broken the back of this production now. We've been here for sixteen shoot days. I'm really in the swing of the walking to set, the saying hello to the miserable Polish concierge, the sitting in the darkened corridor for hours watching the playback monitor, the remembering to hang the improvised cardboard sign on the door with a broken lock when I go to the bog, the eating my lunch in the freezing cold Baptist church hall across the road, the suffering of a Wi-Fi connection that's as slow and erratic as 1990's dial-up. I'm going to miss it all.

Getting out of the apartment also means we've completed all our baby scenes. Get in! They've really come good in the last few days, have the little buggers. I don't quite know how much it's us honing our baby wrangling skills, or them just getting used to being in front of the hot lights, but sod the analysis, we actually managed to capture some golden moments.

We've also finished with one of our main actors. She's been brilliant on and off camera. A real laugh. A special talent and a really special person. She departs with a hug and a promise that I'll chuck some voiceover work her way when I get back to ad land.

We spend the last few hours filming small but important 'pick up' shots in the apartment. (A hand opening a fridge door, a close-up of coffee being poured, shots of the amazing skyline, that sort of thing.) It's our last chance. As soon as we leave, the art department will be getting the rollers out to return our cool pad to its magnolia-hued former self. We end up getting loads of stuff, but while strolling home, I can't help but get that 'did I leave the gas on?' feeling you get in the cab on the way to Gatwick.

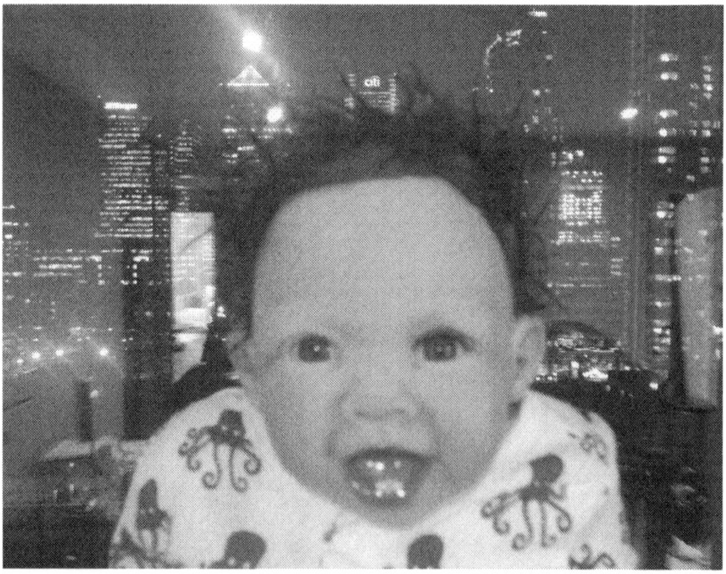

Even Chucky, our stunt baby, is cock-a-hoop.

REALLY GOOD FRIDAY

THE DIRECTOR AND I have just worked out that the last time he or I worked over Easter weekend, I was on a building site and he was doing shifts at a 7Eleven convenience store as teenagers.

Despite the lack of double time on offer, neither of us had any trouble getting our arses to work this morning. I suppose it's because neither of us consider getting brilliant famous actors to burn down a building, 'work'.

We're shooting this boyhood pyro-maniacal fantasy in a builder's yard in the shadow of the West Ham United Olympic Stadium. Apart from the magnificence of the soon-to-be claret and blue fortress, it's a strange area. It's called Hackney Wick; a mixture of canals, newly built flats and old industrial units.

While we wait for the sparks to sort the lighting out, our attention turns to the warehouse opposite. A load of Catweazle-esque bleary-eyed young wastrels keep appearing from inside to look at us. We are as intrigued of them as they are of us. Luckily, our Script Supervisor has a brass neck on her. Before anyone could say 'rat up a drain pipe' she's over there with some story about a film director and screenwriter looking for possible locations and could we have a look?

We step inside. It's an old carpet warehouse that's been converted into some sort of East London live/work space for pretend squatters. It stinks of dope smoke, paraffin heaters and bullshit. These youngsters are paying good money to live in somewhere that is technically uninhabitable. Near where I live, there's a similar warehouse with people living in it. Only those people are eastern European and are squatting there because it is genuinely the only place they can afford.

These kids should be working on a building site or the modern equivalent of 7Eleven, not hanging around making collages or whatever it is they're doing. Sorry, I'm only jealous. I wish that when I was young, I were wealthy enough to be able to pretend I was poor.

We give up trying to comprehend it all and repair to set. It is bloody cold, but the actors are on the money, as always. Damn, our BLA (brilliant leading actress) looks good on camera as she burns down the building.

If he plays his cards right, I reckon my director mate could get a shot at directing London's Burning on the back of this.

PENCIL

TODAY WE'RE ON the thirtieth floor of Millbank Tower, the former HQ of the Labour Party. My grin is as shit-eating as Cherie Blair's as I stroll along the embankment in the morning sunshine on my way to the set. This is the life. The location is to be used as the flash London advertising agency where our lead character works.

The views of London are stunning from up here. And the interior is suitably slick and shiny in a what-the-average-person-would-imagine-an-agency-to-be-like, kind of way. The only thing that our heroine's office is lacking is some advertising awards. The director and I remember this too late. It's a bank holiday weekend, all agencies are shut, and ad awards are not the sort of things that people keep on their mantle pieces at home. Advertising awards need to be on show at work, so everyone knows how brilliant and insecure you are.

The award we particularly want to use is known in the ad business as a yellow pencil. It's the most important. Like an advertising BAFTA award, if you like. Unfortunately, I've never won one, myself. I've won all sorts of others, but never a yellow pencil. I can't even nip over to my office and borrow someone else's.

They've issued new security passes since I've been off, so I have no way of getting in or out of the building. Trying desperately to get my hands on a yellow pencil and not succeeding is the story of my ad career.

However, in the shower this morning I have a brainwave. And as soon as my index finger is dry enough, I text my mate, Julie. She's a pencil winner, but she keeps it at home as she doesn't go in for the whole desk display thing. Not only does she agree to let us borrow her gong, she insists on delivering it to the set in person so she can have a nose about.

Great. A few hurried e-mails to people we know on the board of the awards organisation for permission and the pencil is in the picture. It's in the background, out of focus, but still there for all ad folk to notice. An important touch.

Just because I'm making a movie doesn't mean I don't still have an ambition to win a yellow pencil. Perhaps I should commission a Dye or a Belford (top advertising art director dudes) to knock up a film poster, so I can win one as the client.

LOW LOADER

TODAY'S INSTALMENT IS SPONSORED by The North Face clothing brand. It's not, but it should be. It's eight a.m. Bank Holiday Monday, standing on a street that's been turned into a wind tunnel by the skyscrapers of Canary Wharf. I'm long johned up. It's freezing and completely deserted. Fantastic. These are the perfect conditions to shoot our next scene.

In it, our main character drives to a cash machine at the crack of sparrows to withdraw some money. Trust me, it's a lot more dramatic than it sounds. First, we shoot a wide shot of the car screeching to a halt and our main character getting out and walking to the cash machine. Sounds like a piece of piss. But to make a car screech to a halt on film in exactly the right place takes a lot more welly and skill than you'd think.

Then we shoot the actor and actress talking in the car then her exiting and walking to the cash machine and back. We then swing the camera around and film exactly the same action while lining up on the actor in the driving seat. Then, we shoot the same action again from the perspective of the cash machine.

It's standard stuff, but it still takes the best part of a morning to complete what will end up being about ninety seconds of the film at the very most.

Then, the fun bit. We put the car on a 'low loader', which is basically a very low car trailer that gives the allusion that the car is being driven. This allows us to hang a huge great film camera and film lights on the side of the car while it's moving, and lets the actors concentrate on their acting without any fear of writing off the eighty grand Range Rover that belongs to one of the producers. It's not a big trailer, so while we're filming, only a core essential crew of director, first assistant director, director of photography, camera operator, focus puller, boom operator, sound recorder, script supervisor, make-up lady, wardrobe lady, and director's gimp (me) are allowed on the back of the truck as we tool around East London. Proper movie stuff. I love it.

On today's 'doing stuff you're not allowed to do in adverts' list, we've ticked the not wearing a seatbelt box. And if that wasn't Hollywood enough, when we stop at traffic lights, a gaggle of teenage girls start whooping and waving at our famous leading man in the driving seat. This Bank Holiday Monday beats sitting in a pub getting mullered, hands down.

WILD ANIMALS

WE HAVE HAD EVERYTHING in this production. Sex, violence, stunts, babies, cars, pyrotechnics, and now, wild animals! Pigeons. Two of the little rats avec wings. Okay, they're not man-eating tigers, I grant you, but they are dangerous to the director and I.

Once again, coming from the highly regulated, rigorously positive advertising world means we revel in being able to represent the negative or the subversive in any way shape or form. So, because we can, we've hired a pigeon wrangler to supply us some birds to peck at discarded fast food chicken as an introduction to our drive-thru scene.

The little feathered blighters did what they were supposed to do - be birds that are eating birds - but I must say they were the least hungry pigeons I've ever seen. And I felt like a proper Dick Dastardly when I was helping the wrangler round them up after we'd got the shot.

I suppose this juvenile shot - sorry, artistic symbolism - represents the very reason the director and I started working together on film projects in the first place. Not because we're down on advertising. We're not. It's great. The stamps in our passports prove it. Doing this is just an antidote to our day in the same way that having a nice piece of fish for dinner is an antidote to a butcher's.

Anyway, enough of the cod pigeon philosophy. The simple scene of our two main characters sitting in a drive-thru car park is now up there with my favourites. Neither the director nor myself imagined it would be as poignant and dark-humoured as it plays out. I suppose it was the male character saying all his lines through great big mouthfuls of chicken burger that added a whole extra layer onto it that never quite came across on the page.

The other thing that never came across on the page was the irony of today's schedule that resulted in our actor eating seven and a half chicken burgers while doing the scene this morning, only to be served chicken for lunch.

FALL GUY

I USED TO THINK that being a movie stunt man would be the coolest job in the world. Now I'm knocking on forty, with my love of the hit eighties TV show, The Fall Guy, starring Lee Majors, faded and my knee giving me gyp, I'm not so sure.

Having said that, when I stepped onto set this afternoon and saw the green screen rigged platform with the crash mats and cardboard boxes below (yeah, they really do use cardboard boxes), a jolt of youthful bravado started coursing through my veins. Despite the cold, I suddenly really wanted to give the stunt a try, myself. After all, my party piece as a student was my drunken stuntman roll down the stairs. Aged twenty-one, I fell off a second floor balcony of a Faliraki hotel onto concrete (another story for another book). And I've fallen or have been knocked off my pushbike loads of times. So this stunt is easily within my range.

I make the mistake of voicing my whimsical urge. The assembled crew laugh at me in an 'as if you could double for a twenty-seven-year-old, six foot, athletic young actor with a thick head of dark hair, you twonk' kind of way. Fair point, but I didn't mean actually be the body double, just have a go at the stunt. Both are out of the question. I'm not insured. And anyway, when I stand on top of the platform it's higher than it looks, so sod that daddio.

In the event, to even think for a nanosecond that I could possibly have a go is belittling to the fit, highly trained professionals that do it for a living. They arrive dressed and made up by our peerless make-up and wardrobe people to look like the actors they are doubling for. A team of expert riggers has constructed the set. We have a stunt coordinator and medics on hand. It is a Health & Safety dream, but it's still inherently a bloody dangerous thing to do.

We do two takes. The first take is nailed perfectly. The second is equally amazing, but unfortunately the stunt man hits his head on the way down. We look on, stunned, as the medics and stunt crew rush to his aid. I nearly pass out when the guy's whole scalp comes off in the make-up designer's hand. I regain my composure when I realize it's just a hairpiece. Part of his costume. However, there is a lot of blood (and it has ruined the makeup designer's cashmere mittens, she has asked me to add). An ambulance arrives and he's carted off to the nearest hospital.

We wrap for the day. And it isn't until I get a message in the evening that he's been released from hospital all stitched up, that I feel okay about e-mailing everyone the video of the incident I shot on my phone.

MY BIG MOMENT

NEITHER THE DIRECTOR OR I are what you'd call 'Hitchcockian' filmmakers. By that I don't mean how we make films - although we're not into crash zooms - I mean having the urge to physically appear in all our own stuff, as big Alfred did.

I started my ad career like a wet nosed puppy, quite excited about being in front of the camera. But this was kicked out of me fairly early on when I volunteered to be an extra in a commercial I'd written for a well-known brand of noodles in a pot. Far from lurking in the background, I actually ended up being featured quite prominently. And consequently had the piss ripped out of me for months afterwards by all and sundry.

Today's chance to be featured, however, is something I jump at immediately. The scene takes place on a Docklands Light Railway train where our BLA (brilliant lead actress) has an argument on her mobile phone. I always thought it would be cooler to not hear the person on the other end of the line in this scene, so I only ever wrote our character's side of the conversation in the script. It looks good on the page, but I hadn't realised how unfair it is to expect an actor to pretend to have a convincing conversation without anything to react to. I quickly dash off the other side of the argument and get copies printed and distributed.

We're not allowed to charter our own train for the scene, so twenty of us pile onto the rear carriage of a Lewisham bound train at Bank and we film it in two runs to Island Gardens and back. While we wait for a train, we rehearse the scene. And it is decided that I will play the part of 'Simon' the person on the other end of the phone.

I sit in the next carriage, well off camera (the Simon character is calling from work) and phone her repeatedly for a row. Ten times in a row. Having arguably Britain's finest actress perform my script for the last month has been a heady experience. Actually performing it with her is bonkers. When I say "nice working with you" afterwards and she laughs and sarcastically replies "Loving your work!" I know she's only pretending to rip the piss out of me, and that, actually, she thought I was pretty bloody good.

~~MEAT PUPPETS~~
~~EXTRAS~~
BACKGROUND ARTISTS

IN ALL THE YEARS I've been working on film projects in my spare time, I've tried my best to not go on about it too much. The chances of things like this actually coming to fruition are miniscule, and I didn't want to come across as one of those 'all talk and no action' types. However, as anyone who knows me will attest, I have pretty much failed miserably to not bang on and on about it, ad nauseam. So it's good that what's happened has happened, because it makes me merely a gob-shite, rather than a bullshitting gob-shite.

My family and friends are really excited for me, I can tell. In eighteen years of making commercials, I can count on the fingers on the hand of a man with three fingers the amount of times people have asked to visit a set. During the shooting of this film, I've had nineteen set visits from family and friends. This includes a small speaking part in the film for a former neighbour, a work placement in the wardrobe department for my step-daughter, and 'background artist' appearances for my dad, step-son, step-daughter, step-brother, cousin, nephew, niece, two mates, and two step-children's mates. Blimey, people have been saying I need to get myself an agent. Perhaps I should be an agent.

The scene with all the extras is fun. Cold, but fun. It's a simple scene where our BLA (brilliant leading actress) emerges through the revolving doors of a corporate building, strides across a bustling city square and meets someone she'd rather not. The square is five miles away from where we shot what is supposed to be the interior of the building. (The interior was Millbank Tower by the river near Pimlico, whereas today we're in The City of London.) That's the movies. When I watch the playback monitor during takes, I find myself focusing on the ten smartly dressed friends and family in the background more than the star. I'd feel responsible if any of them spoiled things by looking into the camera and waving.

Another extra I keep an eye out for is Royston. Royston is a little gay dog that belongs to one of the girls in the art department. It has its own Instagram account with 6,128 followers. That's the internet for you. But sod it, that's 6,128 potential cinemagoers, so the dog is in the picture. I resist the massive urge to make my cousin walk him in the scene, and hand the lead to my mate, Ann, instead. It all goes well and everyone enjoys the experience. They'll murder me if they end up on the cutting room floor, though.

I wonder what the collective noun is for film extras?

SCHEDULE

ON A LOW BUDGET FILM like this, the schedule was always going to be tight as a gnat's whatsit. I say low budget. It's a ridiculous amount of cash. In James Cameron/Peter Jackson terms, however, it is a minute or so of screen time. It's also similar in budget to some of the bigger commercials we see on our screens. Plenty of the alcohol/sports/electrical/airline brands spend in excess of the price of a small townhouse in Kensington on their international advertising productions.

I saw one in the cinema the other week that was even more lavish and ostentatious than the jewellery brand it was advertising. A leopard chasing a horse drawn carriage along a nineteenth century frozen River Seine, then running along a mountain range, riding on the head of a three hundred foot elephant with a castle on its back, then hitching a ride on the wing of a Wright Bros biplane across Paris, does not come cheap. I bet the writer of that didn't walk to the set every day. Nor would the schedule be as tight and sometimes as hair-raising as it is for us.

Today, for example, was particularly testing, because it involved shooting in four locations. It was a midday start, shooting an exterior scene in The City of London. All good, except for a bit of snow. (It's April FFS!) Then, while the crew pack everything into the trucks, we shoot some driving shots of our BLA (brilliant lead actress) driving around the city. All good. Then we do a massive unit move from The City to The Isle Of Dogs. A great big caravan of vehicles packing up, moving on, then setting up again. No wonder film productions are likened to circuses. The director and I are the clowns. (There, I said it before you did.)

We drive ahead to the next location, which is a beach. No, I'm serious. There genuinely is a beach on the Isle Of Dogs. We arrive to find the art department already there. They have arranged some detritus on the shore and are really excited because they've found a dead bird washed up. It's a cormorant, according to the director, who is a 'twitcher' on the quiet. I never knew that.

We work out the shots we need. There is no dialogue. It's a wide, a mid-shot and a close-up, plus some cutaways of the dead cormorant. Piece of piss, but it's a day scene and the light is fading. Where the fook are the rest of the crew? We wait. And wait. Apparently, there's been a smash-up somewhere and the traffic is horrific. Of all the rotten luck. We can't not have this scene, man!

Eventually, the circus arrives. Luckily, we don't need to light the scene, so it's just a case of putting the camera on a tripod, loading and shooting. We get what we need just as it's getting dark. Phew.

As we repair to the curry house adjacent for our 'lunch' it's knocking on seven pm and pretty much dark. After a quick cuzza - my order of a chicken cormorant is completely lost on the waiter -

we travel to our final location of the day. It's an exterior night scene in a council estate. F-f-f-f-freezing.

By the time we wrap at eleven-thirty, we are chuffed with what we've managed to cram into the day, but numb with the cold. We make a mental note to wear extra layers tomorrow. As tomorrow is a hyperthermia inducing all-night shoot on the banks of the river Thames. Gulp.

An impromptu prop

LAST DAY

THE FINAL DAY of the shoot is a day off. We're going to be filming all through the night, so the day is mine. I get up at seven am and make the missus a cup of tea. Not really. I lie in until about ten-ish. I get up, shower, breakfast, fart around on t'internet, write an update about stunt men, speak on the phone, get dressed, go for a wander.

I end up in a red French bistro chain restaurant saying the inimitable words: 'Table for one, please'. Seafood bouillabaisse and chips, sorry 'frittes', doesn't go together, but sod it, I'm on a day off. I get my laptop out, so as not to look like a complete loner. I'm aware that it probably makes me look even more of a sado to the mums 'wot lunch', but sod it; I'm on a day off. It's a mantra I repeat to myself as I order a large glass of crisp dry white to accompany my meal.

While I stuff my face, I tap away on my keyboard, finishing an outline for another screenplay I am working on that I need to e-mail to a producer friend this alvo. This is the life. It's like a solo advertising lunch. Except, I'm paying.

Same again with the crisp dry blanc, monsieur. Oh yeah, this is a bit of me, this is. So much so, I really have to force myself to ask for the bill rather than a third bucket of vin. I may be on a day off, but I have an eleven-hour shift tonight.

So I stroll home, and pour myself onto the sofa for some televisual chloroform in the form of Escape To The Country. A tactical kip is imperative if I am to be as fresh a daisy for tonight's final shoot.

LAST NIGHT

I'M REALLY EXCITED and really sad tonight. We're shooting some really cool stuff in a really cool location. We're on the shore of The River Thames. At the part of the river that is right at the bottom of the teardrop of The Isle of Dogs. Oh, you know, the squiggly bit in the middle of the Eastenders map. We've got a lighting rig so big we need a fucking crane to lift it. It's the climax of our filming schedule, but it's also the end. The twenty-seven best days of my life will be over in eleven hours. Sniff.

I turn up at seven pm, as fresh as a daisy. While daylight is with us, we knock off a simple driving sequence. Then, as darkness falls, we set up for tonight. Half the shots in this scene are up on the embankment and half are down on the shore. So we do the embankment stuff first while the tide is high from around nine pm to one am.

I walk along the river all the time, but tonight is the first time I spend so long in one place that I notice how mad the tides are. For the first few hours the water is high, choppy and actually flows upstream. Then, almost imperceptibly at first, the flotsam starts to slide downstream as the tide turns and retreats.

We retreat to the local rowing club, our unit base for the night, for our last 'supper'. I thank the caterers for the half a stone. The director and I eat with our BLA (brilliant lead actress). We thank her for being not only fantastic at the old acting lark, but being a great laugh and a great sport. She's been the complete opposite of a diva, in fact.

It's an attitude that we are about to put to the test in the next few hours. I feel terrible. When I wrote the scene, I had no idea we'd film it in sub zero temperatures. (It's April FFS.) But, regardless, that girl has got to go into the river. It's not the final scene in the movie, but it's the final scene in the shooting schedule. It suddenly dawns on me that it was probably a deliberate piece of scheduling to make the most demanding scene, the last.

In a fit of solidarity, I fling off my toasty North Face thermal boots and don a pair of green rubber waders. 'Fuck it, if you're going in, so am I', I hear myself say. I don't think it helps much. But she does start humming the Smurf tune at the sight of me in waders and a floppy beany hat.

We go back outside, past the cars with iced windscreens (yeah, it's that cold) and down the slipway onto the shore. Two hours ago the water was lapping twenty feet up the embankment wall. It is now sixty feet down the shore and glassy still. Incredible. I feel incredibly privileged to be standing up to my thighs in it at three in the morning.

We've got two cameras. One on a tripod covering a wide angle and the other a 'Steadicam', which allows us to run alongside the actor without the footage being all jumpy. It's crucial to get as much stuff as possible in as short a time, as if we're not careful we'll be in hypothermia territory.

Everyone is cold, tired and tense. We get one great take, but the Steadicam has failed. Of all the rotten luck. We try and keep the actress warm with coats and heaters, but it's her wet feet that are causing her the most discomfort. We sort out the camera problem and go again.

The last part of the scene is her running from the river and up the bank. On the last take, she keeps on running back to her dressing room. And there's a cab waiting with its engine running to whisk her away. Wow. I can't tell you how lucky we are to have had her on board. A-bloody-mazing. The rest of us still have one matter-of-fact shot to cover. We quickly cover it.

AND THAT'S A WRAP!

Hugs, kisses and backslaps are exchanged. Obviously, the rest of the crew are delighted to get another job done successfully. But to the director and I, it is a towering highpoint in our lives.

It's five-thirty in the morning. Nowhere is open. We stroll under the foot tunnel, and when we emerge on the south side at Greenwich, dawn has broken. We take the five-minute walk to my gaff and open the beers. Deserved.

We watch some rushes and reflect on the last few weeks. We've learned a lot. It's been his show, don't get me wrong, but I've been there for every step of the way and I've had a quite a big say. We've had a ball. In twenty-seven days, we only had one minor row. It was about the eye line of one of the actors in one of the scenes. Trivial as anything. And it was on the basement car park day, which was tense as anything because we were behind schedule. Basically, we got on great.

The director bails, pissed and exhausted, at eight a.m. I'm such a lucky boy. Lucky that the script got bought. Lucky that my ad agency allowed me the time off to attend the shoot. Thanks, bosses. Lucky that the director has allowed me on set the whole time and have a creative input. Unlike advertising, writers don't usually get a look in once a film is in production. Many of the crew have told me how rare it is to have a writer on set. So, to make sure I enjoy every moment of this whole experience, I've deliberately treated it like it's never going to happen again. But, bloody hell, I really wish it does happen again.

Anyway, it's not over, yet. Not by a long chalk. The editing and post-production phases are yet to come.

An actor meets a Smurf.

PART THREE
POST-PRODUCTION

INTERROGATION

I'M HAVING A FEW DAYS at home to come down from the intensity and euphoria of the last twenty-seven. My director mate has jetted off somewhere hot. Fair play to him, he deserves it. He has been legendary. Meanwhile, I'm enjoying what every person over the age of thirty considers the height of self-indulgence. I am, of course, referring to the pleasure of lying on one's sofa of an afternoon, watching films, slurping tea and having a snooze. Heaven.

When awake, I'm also indulging in some therapeutic painting sessions. Skirting boards, not still lives. It's good to do something satisfyingly humdrum after the parallel universe of a month I've just had. In that nutty universe I am a proper writer. I hang out with famous actors and talented film-folk every day, and people are interested in what I've got to say. Speaking to PR people and journalists is an everyday occurrence. Well, four times, anyway. And I am name-checked and quoted all over t'internet.

Back in the real world, this perturbs me. I am not what you'd call a PR man's dream. My conversational 'tone of voice' is a mix of cynicism, sarcasm, self-depreciation, piss-take and inarticulateness (see?) that simply doesn't come across when re-quoted in black and white by a journalist. (Which, when I read it back is a roundabout way of admitting that I'm a complete twat.)

I have been interviewed quite a few times in the advertising trade press, but it's never gone that well. On one occasion my oh-so-witty interview replies after winning a (career defining) radio-commercial-of-the-month award were taken so out of context that I had to write a formal letter of apology to be published in the trade magazine and another letter, grovelingly apologizing to the famous comedy actor I had offended.

On set, I was really quite averse to journalists pulling out their Dictaphones and shoving them in my face. So to speak. So far, only one of the articles has been published. It's on a well-known film website. Despite spending a good thirty minutes trying my best to reply to her obtuse line of questioning, I am not quoted. Phew. However, I didn't get away with it completely, because she referred to me in the piece as a 'veteran ad man'. Ouch. That hurts. Especially as, in my parallel movie universe, I am a rookie. A middle-aged, grey-haired, cynical, sarcastic, inarticulate rookie.

BOTTOM DRAWER

I HELPED MY STEPDAUGHTER move out last weekend. (To Dalston, innit.) So the last week has been spent converting her bedroom into an office/spare room. Yes, a bit brutal, but come on, it's not like we've changed the locks.

In the process of de-cluttering our bedroom from an ironing/office/dumping ground into a Zen-like sleeping space, we've emptied quite a lot of drawers. In one drawer I found an early draft of a screenplay. Not for this film we've been making, but the first one I wrote with my director mate.

It's a comedy about a school reunion. We came up with the story in the pubs and curry houses of Soho (as we did with the second one). And then I would go off and spend evenings and weekends crafting it into script form. Not really knowing what I was doing, but kind of applying the scriptwriting principles from my advertising work, then not stopping after one page. Oh and making sure there was loads of swearing in it.

It was good fun, that. At the time I was just doing it for the sake of writing exactly what I wanted to write. Not really with any thought to what it might lead to. Looking back, it was amazing how I managed a nearly half-decent-ish first draft. Especially as I waited until after finishing it before I read a book about how to write a screenplay.

Basically, it turns out I'd approached the thing in exactly the opposite way that you're supposed to. Apparently you're supposed to establish the characters, the beginning, middle and end of the story, and nail a tight page-by-page outline of the story before you start scripting. Then, when you do start writing the narrative and dialogue, you're simply colouring in between the lines of your story.

Our approach was to think of some characters and just write some funny scenes. Then kind of try and knit them all together into a story. Knob heads! So yeah, it was a pleasant surprise, almost a shock, when people who read the first draft seemed to quite like it.

We started to send it to people in the industry. Taking all feedback seriously and re-writing new drafts almost constantly. Somehow, I can't remember how, the script got in front of a Hollywood agent who thought it was hilarious and tender (She wasn't wrong). She thought it was a universal story, (True. Everyone's been to school, right?) And she thought it had a potential to be a hit movie (we lapped this up) and adapted into a musical stage play full of great eighties music. (She lost us with that one.)

She decided to champion the script in order to get us some funding. She tried her best with us two nonentities and she did well. She managed to get the script optioned by some producers*. This was trouser-soilingly exciting for my director mate and me at the time. We got within a whisker of getting the money, too. Well, looking back it might have been a country mile away, but 'within a whisker' is what us two dewy-eyed puppies were told. Whatever, it never actually happened. And eventually the film rights reverted back to us.

We ploughed on. Doing re-writes and sending it off to different people in the film business. One evening, me and my mate were sat in a pub - might have been The Crown and Two Chairmen on Dean Street - bemoaning the fact that our screenplay was getting a lot of negative feedback from film industry people, because they thought it was too smutty. It was probably the Artois talking - or maybe the Guinness - but we suddenly thought it would be a genius idea to change the writer's name on the title page of the script to a woman's. Thus quashing the perceived laddish tone.

We didn't think it through though. Two weeks later, I'm sitting at work trying to think of ideas to sell gravy granules, or some such, and my phone rings. It's someone from a very well known British film institution on the line, asking to speak to Michelle, the writer.

In the split second I have to react, I consider affecting a pretend female voice akin to a Python taking his son to a stoning in Life Of Brian, but think better of it. As I quickly take myself out to the fire escape stairwell for some privacy, I come clean.

It's awkward, but luckily, the guy laughs at our ploy. So a week later, the director and I don't have to wear frocks as we sit in the reception area of the film institution.

The meeting went well. And the subsequent re-writes and meetings. But, needless to say, it never ultimately came to anything. And neither did anything come of the next equally auspicious film institution that we had several meetings with, and did several re-writes for, either.

After seemingly exhausting all further avenues, we came to the conclusion that with a script of this size, tone and ambition, and as complete unknowns with no feature film experience, we were probably never going to get the funding to get it made.

So there was only one thing for it. Well, two things. One was to give up. The other, tougher way to proceed was to get the requisite film experience and profile by writing another, cheaper, simpler film and get it made.

So that's what we did. We put the school reunion comedy in a drawer. And we wrote another one, pared down, not expensive, not smutty, not even a comedy. Written in the correct how-to-write-a-screenplay structure. It turns out its a psychological thriller - other people gave it this genre label, not us. It was the script to this film. And to cut another four-year long story short, here we are.

So you never know, we might end up with a profile enough for the smutty school reunion comedy to be taken seriously. But, first, the current project needs a successful cinematic release, if we are to have a cat in hell's chance. So first things first. Or, second things first, to be totally accurate.

** A 'script option' is the act of buying the rights of a story or script in order to make it into a film. The option to make the script into a film is for a limited time - usually a year or two - in which the producer has the sole right to make the film, should they choose. In that time, they have to get the money together to 'exercise the option' (get the production budget together to make the film) or the script rights revert back to the writer(s).*

CULTURE SHOCK

MY ALARM GOES OFF at a horrendously inappropriate time of the morning with a shrill buzzing noise, which screams: 'Party's over, you chancer! Get your fat arse back to work, where you belong!' Despite numerous snooze button presses, I finally give in to its relentless bullying and get the fuck out of bed. The party is, indeed, over. I've been living the dream for the past five weeks, but now it's time to wake up and smell the office coffee.

To my surprise, in the time I've been away from the agency, they've done away with the crap coffee machines and replaced them with those posh capsule ones. Tick. This isn't the only difference I notice. They've repainted the floor in the reception area. Nice. And for some reason, people are running around looking as stressed and busy as if they were working somewhere really important, like NASA or an emergency brain trauma unit. What's that all about, man? Then I realise. It's advertising. People taking things disproportionately seriously is what it's always like. It's me who's changed, not them. Shit, I'm not going to let myself get stressed out like these cats, daddio. No way.

I saunter to my desk as nonchalantly as I can manage. I am noticed. Everyone seems pleased to see me, and genuinely interested in what I've been up to. Or if not, they are much better at hiding their bitterness and loathing than I would be. I am touched. To the point where I don't mind repeating the same conversation thirty to forty times of how great an experience it was, how quick it's gone, how brilliant and nice the actors were, that we're editing now, and how I'll soon lose the belly once I get cycling to work again, no problem at all.

Of course, my bonhomie is short lived. By the end of day one, I have two briefs on my desk. Both are genuinely great opportunities, which deserve a week's thinking time in their own right. I have a day. I feel like a kid returning to school from the summer holidays who has forgotten how to hold a pen properly. I've just had the longest time of not doing my job since I've been doing my job. And I'm not kidding when I say I have forgotten how to think. I'm a complete jelly head. And I can't keep up with the pace. So I do the sensible thing and partner up with one of the cool young creative dudes in the department. It's the advertising equivalent of an ageing Jan Molby in the Liverpool midfield relying on a young Jamie Redknapp to do his running for him, while he strolls around the park, spraying the Hollywood passes. Kind of. Except I'm not as fat, not as talented, or wealthy, I don't have a ridiculous Danish/Scouse hybrid accent and I do get quicker and more agile as the days pass. By the end of the week, I'm pretty much back up to the speed and seriousness required.

I've picked up the reins of my new chocolate bar account once more. I have missed absolutely eff-all in its development while I've been away. Work has been done on it, but for the life of me, I can't see what. Never mind. It's all good. And I still have an annoying smile on my face that is really pissing off my workmates, because tomorrow morning I have a pre-office-hours meeting to view a rough cut of the feature film. Ding dang do!

ROUGH PEEK

THE DIRECTOR, myself and the editors (we have two of them, so we have) meet up at the crack of sparrows. One of the editors brings the overpriced Soho coffee, I bring the Sausage and Egg McMuffins*. That's the deal. This is going to be the most unusual edit session I've been in.

On a TV commercial, the editor spends a couple of days compiling footage into a rough assembly. Then the director joins in for a day or so until they have a cut they are happy with. Then, the 'agency' is invited in - copywriter, art director, agency producer - and a further fiddle is had. In my experience this can range from looking at a few alternative takes that you remember liking from the shoot, to having to roll up your sleeves and bully the director and editor into making the thing actually make sense. Whatever, it is a chance to really indulge in minutiae; to watch the ad thirty-plus times, to try different versions, to lose twenty-six frames by shaving one frame from each shot until it fits into thirty seconds, to send out for sushi, to make the product shot longer, and longer.

This is a different animal. The editors have had a full two weeks to get to this point (with a few days of the director's input). You can't watch a feature-length movie thirty times back-to-back.

Kubrick probably did, but he didn't have a full day at the office ahead of him. So we play the film once from start to finish, without stopping, and make notes along the way for the editors to then address later. Like any rough cut, the picture doesn't look great, the sound is rough, and the post (special effects) work is yet to be done. Unlike an ad rough cut, there are blank gaps where we need to go out with a camera and shoot some more second unit stuff**.

Despite this, I am glued to the screen. I've seen some scene assemblies already, but not all strung together as a whole. The editors have added loads of music, which I am not expecting. It's a pleasant surprise. Some of it's by a famous electronic artist, and the rest by a film score composer dude we like. It's really dark stuff that adds an intense psychological element to the mood. I love it. We won't use this actual music in the finished film, but it certainly makes for a brilliant brief for whomever we commission to compose the score (maybe the same composer dude we have used for the placeholder music).

Ninety-six minutes later, it's over. My list of notes is only a page long. I'm chuffed, particularly as only one of my suggestions is met with derision by the others. I'm sure we'll end up getting really anal on everything in due course. Hope so. There's plenty of time in the schedule for that. And it won't include time spent responding to creative director comments, account director comments, client comments, senior client comments, client's wife's comments, the whole of the client marketing department's comments, Clearcast comments. Basically, a hell of a lot of comments which, as you go further down the list, get more ridiculous and more likely to mess up your ad. Having said that, I'm new to this film lark. For all I know, there could be just as many people with agendas in film, too, but with different job titles. We could be backwards and forwards forever. My McMuffin bill could run into hundreds. I'll let you know how we get on.

The back of editor Scott's head.

**Other fast food breakfasts are available. They are not nearly as good, though. Seriously, why the hell they don't roll out the breakfast menu all day long is beyond me. You are missing a trick there, Ronald.*

***They are called 'second unit' shots; because on big films they have a second film unit whose job it is to pick up incidental shots that don't involve actors.*

SHOWING THE PRODUCERS

I'M BACK AT THE EDITORS'. It's after office hours, not before, so the McMuffin budget is not dipped into. We're here to show the producers the assembly cut for the first time. I feel the same nervousness that I do when presenting a rough cut to an advertising client. Not that I think of our producers as clients, you understand. Well, kind of, I suppose. They sign all the cheques, like a client. But I respect the creative opinions of these guys more than any Marketing Director I've met. After all, they bought into our script and they bought into us as the people to bring it to the screen. They gave us good notes to help us tighten the story. Then found a huge amount of money and assembled a highly talented team of actors and technicians to make it all happen. All in all, they've shown an incredible amount of faith in a pair of advertising ne'er-do-wells. So, yeah, I'm nervous because I really want them to be pleased with what they see. Besides, on any project you work on, regardless of the industry, it's always a more enjoyable experience, often with better end results, when all members of the team are pulling in the same direction. So, for me, tonight will set the tone for the rest of the post-production process.

We settle down with our imaginary popcorn and watch. All comments from the other day's session have been addressed. It's getting better.

After ninety-five minutes the producers give us a round of applause. Bloody hell. They are happy bunnies. They have comments, of course. So does every person in the room. It's great, because everyone's comments are constructive and thought through. Even mine.

One thing the producers raise (and the director and I agree with) is that the music is a bit much in places. Funny, I raved about it after the first viewing, but I'm not so sure about it now. Fickle fucker that I am. Part of it is because it is crudely applied, unmixed. Part of it is because it's not designed specifically for the pictures. And the other thing is, it makes it all a bit full-on David Lynch. Not a bad territory, but certainly not what we were aiming for. Tonally, we're going for just the right balance of artistic integrity and bums-on-seats popularity. Films have to make money, after all. So, although the music must be powerful enough to help drive the narrative, it shouldn't actually give people a headache, either. Fair point.

LEGAL DOWNLOAD

I DON'T DO the whole illegally-downloading-films-from-the-internet thing. Not for any strongly held protection of copyright beliefs. I'm sure in the future, when it's my film getting pirated, I will find it as abhorrent as a wisp of Lambert & Butler fume in the nostril of an ex-smoker. But, for now, it is purely down to my lack of technological on-the-ball-ness.

However, I have been downloading rough cuts of my film over the last few days. I'm either doing something wrong or it genuinely does take about three hours every time. Jesus. And the system of file sharing we're using for said transfers, doesn't help, either. If you don't download in a certain way, the movie is actually wiped off the shared folder and the rest of the team can't access it. It does whenever I do it, anyway. Apparently, it's hugely annoying for the rest of team. One has been hauled over the coals by one's colleagues for this act. And further reminded that one must, under no circumstances, share the file with anyone else.

They have no fears on that one. The first time I'll be sending people links to this movie will be an Amazon link to the DVD. This is not a pirate film, in either a genre or lack of royalties in writer's pocket sense. Having said that, I have always said to the director that I'll know we have cracked it when the little Chinese woman who sells dodgy DVDs in the pub I drink in after West Ham games offers me my own movie for '£3 or two for a fiver'.

QUALITATIVE RESEARCH

THERE'S NOTHING TO SEND a shiver down the spine of a creative person in advertising more than the word 'research'. That, and the word 'client'. Oh, and also the words 're-brief' 'Clearcast' and 'tissue', of course*.

Okay, there are a lot of sphincter-tightening words, but 'research' is probably the worst Pavlovian bottom clencher of the lot. Part of the reason for embarking on an extra-curricular creative endeavor in the first place was as an antidote to the paper cuttery of research in one's day job. Most ad creatives worth their salt have a creative sideline, which at the very least helps them retain their enthusiasm for, and become better at, their jobs. On occasion it can even lead to a second career. Just out of the creative partners I have worked directly with over the years, one is a published novelist, one's a fine art photographer and art magazine publisher, one's a fashion shop owner and one's an artisan printmaker. All very different and interesting pursuits in their own right. But trust me to be the only one whose sideline still involves bloody research.

Yesterday we had the first of a series screenings to gauge from audiences just how the film is shaping up in order to help us craft just the right finished product. This one we call a 'dinner party screening', where we invite a small number of people to watch the film in its unfinished state, then pick their brains about it over dinner, afterwards. How civilized? In advertising, this approach is known as 'qualitative research'**. And if this hasn't got the old clacker going enough, the invited guests are all respected professionals from the film industry. Fuck. In advertising it's usually housewives, but we've got a respected writer, a big-time producer, a respected film editor, a top art director and a well-known actor sitting down to look at our rough cut in a Soho screening room. So it makes it more like the showing of an unfinished ad to a particularly steely awards jury.

Terrifying. But it does have its plus points. When discussing an ad, the housewives usually get Twiglets and cheap chardonnay to help the conversation. Being the movies, we repair for dinner at Soho House for our post-match analysis. And thankfully, the bonhomie extends itself to the feedback, too. The consensus is that we're in good shape considering how early we are in the process. And they all give some valuable pointers as to how to tighten/dramatise/clarify our story further. Which, believe me, is a lot more useful that what you get from Mrs. A.N. Other of Orpington after a half a bottle of free plonk.

** Client = The people who work in the marketing departments of the brands that advertising agencies work for. 'The client has just blown out that brilliant script you wrote'.*

Re-brief = When an ad campaign is presented to the client and they don't like it, the agency then re-briefs their creative department (with client feedback) in order to generate another, more client-pleasing, ad campaign. 'It's a re-brief, I'm afraid. The client absolutely hated the work'.

Clearcast = The UK advertising regulatory body that makes sure every commercial that goes on UK television is fair, accurate and has acceptable levels of taste and decency. 'Clearcast won't let the ad go on air, because, apparently, that goldfish bowl in the background of the scene doesn't have an air pump filter, and therefore, is considered cruel to the fish.'

Tissue = A 'tissue meeting' is a meeting in the early stage of a project in which initial ideas are shared with client for their feedback. (Not a polished presentation, but just some ideas that can easily be screwed up and tossed away, like tissue paper.) 'Even though it's a tissue meeting, the client is expecting ten completely thought through and fully executed ad campaigns'.

*** Qualitative Research is research that uses a small amount of respondents, allowing the time to get a large amount of in-depth, quality feedback from them. Whereas 'quantitative research' reaches a large quantity of people, but only allows a certain amount of questions to be asked. If you've ever been asked to fill out a questionnaire, that's quantitative research.*

MINUTIAE

A QUARTET OF YOUR FINEST Sausage and Egg McMuffins, my good man - say I. I'm on my way to another pre-office hours edit session. What with the day job, I haven't managed to get to the editors' much, lately, apart from for WIP (work in progress) screenings. It's been frustrating to miss out on all the fun. Great strides have been made with the cut. But apart from written notes sent to the director after every viewing, I've had minimal involvement in its progress. So I have a spring in my step as I approach the innocuous door in the one remaining seedy part of Soho, brown paper bag in hand.

The pretty young receptionist is really pleased to see me. Not because it's me, but because one of the editors has already eaten breakfast, so she gets to stuff her face with the spare McMuffin. I iron mine out in the windowless edit suite. And we start going through stuff. The cut has been worked on for about a month now. As far as we're concerned, the pace and feel are really starting to work well (but we would say that). Especially in light of all the comments the guys have taken on board in the last week, or so. They've done a cracking job, because despite all the work, many of the changes are pretty imperceptible. But the net result is a more pleasing narrative.

This type of immersion in storytelling you simply do not get to do in commercials. All of us in the room are from the advertising world. So we are all finding this longer process equally, in the words of Danny Dyer, 'as sweet as a fackin' nut'.

I have four or five things that I want to look at while I'm here today. None are structural; just things that bug me. Minutiae stuff. Some of them bug me, but nobody else. But I'm the writer, so I'm really particular about the intonation of all the delivered dialogue. I make the guys go through all the takes of a few different scenes to find alternatives that are just right.

One of the things I want to improve is a throwaway line that delivers an important bit of the plot. So it is extra critical that it doesn't stick out like a dog's doodah.

It's not easy trying to evaluate nuances of intonation. Especially when it's to a soundtrack of pneumatic drilling. The premises below the editors' offices is being transformed from a sex shop to a coffee shop. Obviously, it's fantastic news that Soho is getting another much-needed coffee outlet, but it's doing our ears in.

Despite this, we manage to fix the dialogue. The rest of the room didn't have a problem with it, as was. But the director says he is gutted to admit that it is far better thanks to my belligerence. Get in. Those eighteen years of directing advertising voiceover artists to say things like 'nutritious and delicious' sixty-seven different ways, have not been completely in vain*.

* *The average voiceover recording session goes like this:*

"That's great, Now let's try it again with a bit more emphasis on the 'and'... Superb, but I'm not really hearing the smile in your voice. Let's go again... Okay, we've got that. What's your natural accent, by the way..? West Country. Cool. Let's have a bit of that coming through this time.... Okay, that was a mistake. You sound retarded. Let's go back to the RP accent.... Great. Now try it more intimately, like you're confiding in one person... ... Brilliant, but don't forget that smile, and the pause between 'and' and 'delicious' that I like... Fantastic. Okay, loving what you're doing. Now let's just try some wild takes of the word 'delicious'... Hmm, try it more like 'Deeelicious!'... And again... Once more... 'Der-liciousssss!'... We've got it! Thank you! We'll use 'nutritious' from take seven, the 'and' from take twenty-six, and 'delicious' from take sixty-five".

QUANTITATIVE RESEARCH

IF EVEN SIX MONTHS AGO you'd told me I would be sitting in a packed cinema at BAFTA, the home of British film, alongside two hundred and twenty-six other people, watching a screening of my own film, I would have said "Bloody hell, that's a long opening sentence, call yourself a wordsmith?"

I would have also scarcely believed that such an event would ever come to pass. Well, last night it did. But it wasn't the dewy-eyed triumph that I would have dreamed it to be. In fact, it was excruciating. It was a test screening of the film in its horrendously unfinished state. The look of the film is unset, the sound is all over the place, the music is placeholder stuff, the post-production effects haven't been applied, the titles haven't been designed, and there are still some shots we need to go out and shoot. So showing it to such a large audience (a proportion of which being friends and family) went against every sinew of my person.

The missus said I looked paler than a disgraced nineteen-seventies TV personality in front of a news crew as I greeted everyone at the pub beforehand. And things didn't improve that much during the screening. I reckon I could have skipped around the packed theatre bollock naked and not felt any more exposed.

Jesus, it was tough. But funnily enough, watching it in front of so many others, feeling their reactions, does throw into focus all the bits that need looking at. And, pleasingly, the bits that are working well.

We asked everyone to fill out a questionnaire afterwards. It's called quantitative research, as you well know. But even before the person who drew the short straw from the production team is able to collate the data, we're cracking on with the changes. Basically, it's too slow at the front and a couple of the performances need toning down. The music's wrong and two or three of the moments that we hoped would get a big audience reaction but didn't, we re-cut to make stronger. Well, we'll see about that on our next round of 'quant' in a few days, where we screen it to another audience. And I do another few laps of the theatre with my cock out*.

* *Metaphorically.*

HOT HOUSE

THEY SAY NOTHING GOOD ever comes of overthinking. It's true. It doesn't. You'd probably say that all this research we're doing is overthinking. Well let me tell you, our film research activity is a mere passing whimsy next to the rigorous brain bleed of the advertising research programs my commercial work has to go through.

Our chocolate bar client loves research. Loves it. Most clients do. I think it's because marketing is a quasi-science. It attempts to objectify and make the act of selling people shit they don't need into some data driven science.

Unfortunately for them, the bit that I do - the coming up with the creative work - is subjective. Creative types have a good gut for knowing what's good and what ain't. And a good ad can add many zeros to the profits of a brand and give marketing people fat bonuses and better company cars to drive around in.

However, marketing people are not creative and do not possess a good gut. At all. So they spend a lot of effort, and a heck of a lot of money, trying to objectify the subjective in order to plan themselves a successful advertising campaign.

Our chocolate bar client has enlisted the help of a top (for 'top' read 'top dollar') research company to help us devise exactly the right strategy to deliver great advertising to the snackers of the western world (for 'the western world' read 'The UK, Germany. Israel, Australia and New Zealand markets'.)

They won't take my word for what's good. They need scientific proof, don't you know. So we have handed our thinking to the research company to test with consumers. And today the research people have invited the clients and us agency people to an all day 'hothouse' session where they present their findings. They could present their findings over email, of course, but an all-day meeting in a flash conference room with posh coffee and artisan sandwiches lends more weight and significance to telling us what people think of chocolate bars.

I don't care if I have to be on my best behavior in front of clients, I refuse to take this shit seriously. Everything about it makes my skin crawl. From the 'ice breaker session' at the beginning where everyone in the room has to introduce themselves and say what their dream alternative career would be, to the way the bloke moderating the session writes key words on his flip chart with his squeaky fucking pen. And I especially hate the way he seems to have his own made up Americanized (spelt with a zed) vocabulary.

To amuse myself, every time he says a bullshit word or phrase I jot it down. Here is the list...

Brand champion
Biophilia
Cultural meme
Annual dip

Health lexicon
Spike
Innately new
Motivational territory
Vitality space
Pull an emotional lever
Natural base
End end benefit
Security control space
Deprivation exercise
Category language
Creative fuel
Intentionality
Nomadic cells
Deep dive
Step change
Holistically whole
Ladder up
Connective tissue

Seriously, I'm not making it up. (You couldn't make this shit up, as they say.) Remember, this is a meeting about chocolate bars, not some world-leading think tank on ending world poverty. So the jargon is neither welcomed nor understood. Not at my particular corner of the vitality space, anyway.

Although, as the day goes on, and we huddle in both breakaway pods and as a holistically whole team to deep dive into certain motivational territories in the health lexicon in order to find some kind of cultural meme we can pour creative fuel upon, the intentionality of this particular category language starts to pull an emotional lever and I begin to understand the end end benefit of this whole deprivation exercise. That is, to blind us with science in order to justify their fee.

Well, I'm not blind. So it's lucky for them, that despite the holistically whole load of bollocks of the delivery, their findings did actually concur with my gut feel about chocolate bar adverts. And I didn't have to pour creative piss on their dubious intentionality.

But, by Christ, I need a beer afterwards.

QUANTITATIVE ROUND TWO

ANOTHER CINEMA, another test screening. We're not at BAFTA this time, but a private cinema in Soho. There's nothing seedy about this. It's a cinema that is specifically for film industry screenings, okay? So there will be no nakedity. Not even metaphorical nakedity from myself.

Although I am a bit nervous, it is nothing compared to the first test last week. For a start, I haven't invited anyone I know this time (apart from the missus and the kids). Also, we've spent the week addressing the issues that came out of the first screening, so we're looking forward to seeing if they've done the trick.

Thirdly, it's my fortieth birthday* today, so I have been in the pub since lunchtime. In fact, I only went back to the office for birthday cake and champagne with one's colleagues. (Did I mention I work in advertising?) So I'm in 'high spirits' as I sip my pre-screening plonk in the foyer. It's an odd feeling sitting in a theatre full of people while one's work is displayed. I become acutely aware of the crowd, sensing their reactions, feeling their restlessness at certain times, and picking up when they are absorbed and when they are not.

Knot in stomach aside, it's actually a really worthwhile thing to do, this audience testing, because it helps us see the flaws and the strengths so much more clearly than when viewing it just with the other people working on it. Then again, it could just be because I'm pissed. Either way, it feels better this time. And the bit I observe of the post-screening audience discussion, led by one of the producers, seems to back that feeling up.

However, I don't get to stay to the end. I've booked a table somewhere posh, so me, the missus and kids have to leg it.

"Bring me a dozen of your finest oysters, my good man..." I say. "How much..? Okay, make that a half a dozen of your second finest oysters, then".

The cinema is full, so muggins has to sit on the floor.

** Yes! I got a movie shot before the age of forty! Sadly, I didn't get to play for West Ham United in that time. However, Billy*

Bonds and Teddy Sheringham both turned out for the mighty hammers in their fifth decade. So I shouldn't give up on that dream completely.

PICK UPS

TODAY, WE GO OUT and shoot all the shots we didn't cover off during 'principle photography'. These are 'pick-ups' - shots we need to pick up - that, now we've got the edit pretty much sorted, we've realized we need. You never shoot pick-up shots in commercials. There is always a fixed air date you're working to, so there is never time to fanny about filming extra stuff. In the movies, however, it's not unusual to go back and film whole scenes again. Sometimes actors are even re-cast in certain roles and reshot.

Thankfully, ours is incidental stuff that doesn't require any actors. So there's no accompanying circus of wardrobe, make-up, sound recordists, lighting electricians, art department, runners, catering etc.

All that are present today is the director, the camera operator, camera operator's assistant, a producer and an assistant producer. And a camera. And me. I reckon this is probably the first time in movie history that the writer is present on a pick-up shoot. But I have a day off work today*. And it's near my house, so I'm joining in. I am acutely aware of the incongruity of my attendance, so I've already volunteered myself a technical role to justify it: That of 'Shoe Wrangler'.

Our first shot of the day is of a training shoe being washed up on the riverbank. I'm the mug, sorry, technician who is going to wade in up to his knackers to retrieve it after every take. (On a regular shoot day, a proper props person would be doing this.) It's the end of May and we're conscious that the season has changed since we finished principle filming. There are now leaves on trees and flowers have burst open. So we need to be careful where we point the camera.

Luckily, it's an absolutely atrocious day. It's windy and pissing down with rain, so in keeping with the cack weather we had in March and April. But Jesus, the river is cold. And the director, producer and cameraman take delight in making me throw the shoe out into the river then wade out and retrieve it. Much further out than I suspect I need to from their laughter.

We get the shot, so I get out of the Thames and towel myself down. The rest of the shots we need are of a car driving around, some angles on the river and some cityscapes. Nice photography stuff. But most of it is at night, which is over four hours away. My work here is done. I let the rest of the skeleton crew to go back to our main location on the Isle Of Dogs and I cycle home to greet my party animal mates who are down from Scotland for a weekend of party animaling. Bring it on.

A wrangled shoe.

A film crew laugh at a shoe wrangler.

* *It is the weekend of my 40th birthday bash. I have various family and friends arriving for the weekend to drink me out of house and home.*

QUANTITATIVE ROUND TROIS

I'M JUST ABOUT The only person on this packed commuter train who has a smile on his face as it trundles out of Kings Cross. As well as high-fiving myself for living in London, I am looking forward to tonight's third and last test screening of the rough cut. I haven't confirmed this with the producers, but I am assuming the reason for screening the film in the town of Hitchin, Hertfordshire, is to see how it goes down in a cultural desert. So here I am on the ten past six, full of snoring and farting world-weary commuters. (Ticket paid for out of my own pocket, I hasten to add.)

Doing research groups in different places is perfectly normal. Many's the time I've had my advertising dreams shattered by the ill-informed opinions of the housewives of Basingstoke, Sheffield, Swindon, Huddersfield...*

This week I had to sit through a live video link to a room full of obese middle-aged women in Australia as they rejected six months of my work on chocolate bars. Even the research company didn't see that coming. The wonders of technology, eh? Shame our train network isn't as technologically wonderful. It takes twenty minutes longer than timetabled to get to Hitchin.

Nevertheless, after being met at the station by a childhood pal (who lives in the area) we still make it to the local college theatre in time for a couple of plastic glasses of supermarket rouge. The theatre holds a hundred and fifty. It's a full house. The director's not here tonight, but both editors, two producers, the writer, and half a dozen or so of the writer's family and friends are. (My mate and his workmate, my dad and step-mum, another friend and her dad and step-mum.) And one of the editors has invited quite a few from the local garage where he gets his Maserati serviced. (We're from advertising, baby.)

I was nervous at the first test, half-cut at the second, but tonight I am perfectly lucid and relaxed. Bar a little fiddling, we're pretty much there with the cut. So tonight, for me, is just seeing if the improvements we've made this week work okay, and if the pick-ups we shot slot into the edit well. It's all good. The consensus is positive and the added bonus is we get to miss the England football friendly on TV. We head to the nearest boozer to celebrate. And I just about make the last train back to civilization before I turn into a bumpkin.

**...Dublin, Dundee, Humberside. Hang the housewife, hang the housewife, hang the housewife, HANG THE HOUSEWIFE, HANG THE HOUSEWIFE, HANG THE HOUSEWIFE, HANG THE HOUSEWIFE. Hang the housewife, hang the housewife, hang the housewife, HANG THE HOUSEWIFE...*

Ahem... Sorry. I'm not bitter, or anything.

LOCKDOWN MEETING

ANOTHER MCMUFFIN MORNING. I've overbought again. The director reckons he has had muesli already, and for some strange reason, our sophisticated Parisian female Producer doesn't want hers, either. Fair enough on her part, but I am disgusted that the director has turned his back on his Ilford roots so brazenly. However, I have no time to force him to eat it, or even barrack him verbally, as we need to get going.

This is the 'lock down meeting'. We're in the edit suite. It's the last week allowed in the schedule for editing. So after all the shaping, honing and fiddling, and the feedback from our various private and public screenings ringing in our ears, we need to formally agree the last little bits to be done. So, by the end of the week, we can have a final cut of the film that we can lock down for the postproduction work*. It's a meeting consisting of six people: the director, both editors, both producers and myself. Once again, the writer almost never gets into meetings like this, so I am well aware of how lucky I am. But it's not to say I sit in the corner like a dewy-eyed puppy. I have strong opinions, albeit lightly held. We all do. Everyone has their own little list of things they want to look at. And quite often there is disagreement. But I notice that even when someone in the room is in a minority of one, the others give them a fair hearing. And most ideas are at least tried. Nothing is dismissed out of hand, and in fact, some ideas turn out to work in the cut, despite the consensus of the room being that they wouldn't. I'm gladdened by this 'suck it and see' approach. It is honest and grown up, and not what the director or I are used to.

I'm sorry to report that neither the shot of the dead cormorant, nor the 'shoe floating in the river' scene made it into the final cut. I feel for the cormorant. And it means I don't get a credit in the movie as shoe wrangler. Gutted. But that's the movies. Sigh.

After the meeting, the director reminds me that getting a final approved edit of a commercial often involves having to do some insane changes mandated by the client that makes a creative person want to harm a small defenseless animal. And that this is a walk in the park in comparison.

He's right. But it's okay for him. He's a muesli-eating movie director, lounging around in an edit suite all day. I'm a McMuffin-munching copywriter with a day's work at the office ahead of him. It's an office where one of my colleagues keeps a pet gerbil and lets it run around in its little ball all day. Now, I have been conditioned my whole life to kick spherical objects that roll towards me. It has been quite a test of self-restraint at times, let me tell you.

A gerbil in an office. Yes, a gerbil in an office.

** The edit is part of the post-production process, as it is done post the production (the shoot). But it's only the other stuff like the sound, the grade, the post and the music score that are generally referred to as 'post production'. I really don't know why. Answers on a postcard, s'il vous plait.*

PICTURE LOCK

I HAVE LEARNED a valuable lesson about writing a published diary today. That is, if you're going to give it the big one in a public arena, even just for comedic effect, you can't afford to put a foot wrong yourself.

I realize this precisely one second after pulling the fruit salad from my rucksack in the edit suite. Before I can explain my hangover and my need for healthy intake, the director proceeds to give me some I-can't-believe-you-slagged-me-off-for-eating-muesli-you-double-standards-ponce kind of abuse.

It's a fair cop. Hopefully, the only disagreement of the day. We're here to review all the changes made since the Lockdown Meeting and agree the final edit of the film. We do. Everything that's been done has worked and everyone is all smiles, handshakes and air kisses. Cool. I only have two ridiculously miniscule changes. One of them is to cut away from a shot twelve frames earlier (half a second). The other is to put in a two second pause before a line of dialogue. The editor has another half a dozen tiny changes of his own and we're done. It's been eight weeks. We've had four test screenings and numerous private ones. The editors have been really brilliant in the way they've cut the film, but also handled all the egos involved in a way that made everyone feel listened to and involved. Not least the mouthy writer with ideas above his station.

This last week could have been stressful, but it wasn't thanks to them and the director. In fact, the only downer was courtesy of a famous person.

In one of my favourite scenes, two of the characters dance and sing in a kitchen, pissed, to an upbeat anthemic track. I'd written the tune specifically into the scene. We'd shot it with the actors singing along to it. And we had agreed a fee for its usage with the record company. We just needed the writer of the track – an icon of British music who will remain nameless – to allow us to use his *song, too.* Easier said than done. Apparently, he thinks *modern life is rubbish* and so never uses e-mail. Despite help from the record company, *there's no other way* we could contact him for four months. Until this week we heard he'd finally logged into his e-mail account and given us *the universal* no. How *dare* he?

I wouldn't mind, but he didn't even watch the film before deciding. Fair enough if we were a commercial. Loads of artists don't like seeing their work appearing in ads over *coffee and TV.* But this is a film, man. How about some championing some young filmmakers? (All right, middle-aged.) We have a quick think to see if we know anyone who knows him personally. Even though none of us are as famous as *Clint Eastwood,* it turns out one of the editors has a mutual friend, so we're going to give it a go. Worth a try, but we can't *park life* completely in the meantime, because we may end up being the *last living souls.*

We've had to recut the action, so the *girls and boys* dance in the scene, but not sing along to the music. We're proceeding like we'll never get the original track approved. But we're hopeful we can reason with him. After all, he is the same age and grew up only a few miles away from the director. They probably both eat muesli for breakfast. Although, I suspect that he might prefer to start a *day on All-Bran.*

POST

I'VE BEEN SNOWED UNDER at work this week. Outrageous. How dare they get their money's worth out of me? Working late every day does nothing for the social life, you know. Nor is it conducive to one's involvement in one's first feature film. Are the Coen Brothers ever one short, because one of them has to bust his gut on an advertising new business pitch? No, they are not. But the director and I are not the Coen Brothers. We are more like the Chuckle Brothers*. So it's up to me (to you, to me, to you...) to knuckle down while the director continues on our labour of love.

It's not the end of the world. Now the edit is finalised, a bit of the pressure has lifted. And so it's great to hear the director being so relaxed as he fills me in over the phone about everything that's going on.

All our post work is being done through a company called Technicolor**. This is a bit cool in itself, as it's a real *movie* post house. My mate's met the sound engineer and briefed in all the sound. This includes all the sound effects to add, the stuff that needs cleaning up or accentuated and our ADR brief (Additional Dialogue Recording). I love this part of production. In another life, I reckon I'd have liked to have been a sound engineer. Some of my most enjoyable moments in advertising have been spent dicking about in sound studios. Although my days of inserting subliminal messages into radio ads for fast food chains are behind me, I still find it a laugh. But another aural part of the process – the music score – I'm not so confident with.

I find briefing/directing composers quite difficult and the results really varied. And that's just for thirty-second pieces of music. A ninety-three minute score is a hugely complex and involved undertaking. So it's fantastic that we've managed to get an Oscar-winning composer to work with us. My mate met and briefed him and said it went really well. I wish I were there. Particularly for the moment when the composer said he'd need a forty-piece string orchestra to bring the score to life properly, and the colour drained out of the producer's face.

I'm going to have to book a few days holiday time from the office, because there's no way I'm missing that recording.

Forty strings! Proper.

** Nickname given to us by our BLA (brilliant lead actress). I am taking it as a term of endearment.*

*** Remember all those amazing old films that used to say 'Filmed in Technicolor' in the credits? Well Technicolor was the company whose process was used in the first colour movies like The Wizard Of Oz, Snow White etc etc. The company is still going strong as a movie post-production facility. They do big shit, like Avatar. And now, our humble offering, too.*

DRIVE THRU

ONE OF THE SCENES in the film involves the two main characters pulling into a drive-thru for food*. Due to the filming policies of the fast food behemoths we ended up shooting said scene, not in a genuine drive-in restaurant, but in an Asda car park on the Isle of Dogs.

Our makeshift burger joint was contrived from a combination of MDF, a couple of light-boxes with pictures of burgers on, some carefully placed pot plants and some helium-filled balloons. Shit as that sounds, it looks surprisingly convincing on screen, as it goes. (Big up da art department. Brrrrap, brrrap!) But it meant that when the actor wound his window down and placed his order through the speaker, he was only talking to the script supervisor, hiding behind a pot plant. We were never going to use her voice in the finished film. Excuse the sweeping generalization, but you don't tend to get forty-something Notting Hillbillies working in East London burger joints. Having said that, my Big Issue seller has one of the poshest voices I've ever heard. You would never cast him as a Big Issue seller in a film though, as nobody would believe someone who speaks like that would be on his uppers.

On that basis the editor's forty-something dulcet tones that we used as a placeholder in the rough cut are no more appropriate. So now we're onto the stage in the process where we're building the final sound for the film, we have to get the young and spotty real thing. (I know, you can't hear spotty, but you know what I mean.)

One of the producers put his teenage daughter forward, but as the actor calls the person 'boss man' in the scene, it needs to be delivered by a bloke.

The director asks me if I know anyone who fits the bill. We're not looking for a thespian for this role, just a young bloke with a London accent. We have a sound studio at work, so I agree to get it recorded, my end, and send the file to the sound engineer at Technicolor. However, I quickly realise that this being an ad agency, the pool of young blokes with non-posh accents isn't Olympic-sized. Plus, it's a sunny Friday afternoon and all the management are away at the Cannes Festival (there's an advertising one, as well as a film one. Jesus, there must be a lot of rich cocaine dealers in Cannes). So the agency is like the effin Marie Celeste.

I wander around the building looking for likely candidates. All the pwoppa geezers in the facilities department have done one. Shit. I even consider asking a complete stranger in the street when I pop out for a coffee. Too weird. Eff that. I'm about to give up when I bump into a young bloke who has just started in the IT department. Luckily, my Saville-esque opening gambit of 'Would you like to be in a movie?' didn't freak him out, and the next thing is, I'm sitting in the sound recording booth directing him to say 'Do you want fries with that?' sixty-seven different ways. Boom. Saved the production a few bob, there. And young matey has got my back next time my e-mail is on the blink. It's a win/win.

* *I've already gone on about the drive-thru scene in sections called 'Art Department' and 'Wild Animals'. Go on, have a look if you don't believe me.*

REDEMPTION SONG

OF ALL THE AMAZING musical geniuses to have been spawned by the loins of this small, yet culturally virile nation of ours, there is one who stands on stage head and shoulders above his venerated peers.

For, having founded one of the most successful bands to ever grace our Great British pop charts, he then proceeded to reinvent the idea of the pop group with a band made entirely of two-dimensional musicians.

Three glorious albums ensued with this comic book beat combo, fusing the most diverse genres into a seamless parallel universe of a sound that succeeded in walking the catchy/sophisticated tightrope to delight the popistas and the musos alike.

If his imagination is gargantuan - and it is - it is more than matched by his reserves of positive energy. But he expends it not on the trivial machinations of the music business. By wisely eschewing the constraints of modern social technology he exists in an impenetrable bubble of creativity, free to push himself and, therefore, British popular music as a whole, in yet more exciting and diverse directions. Not as an ego driven limelight addict, but as an artist.

Whether he's assembling supergroups, revisiting former glories, composing operas, or reviving the fortunes of the artists he collaborates with, his talent and generosity is seemingly boundless.

This supreme altruism was demonstrated most recently, when he turned his wondrous blue eyes to film. Where, after watching a rough-cut version of a debut British independent movie, he was impressed enough to grant permission for a track of his to be used, incidentally, in one of the scenes.

The filmmakers were delighted and thankful that his kindness had transformed the scene from good to great. And those naysayers who questioned his credentials as a genuine colossus amongst men, now didn't *Dare*.

ADR

AFTER A DAY OF CHOCOLATE BAR script writing, I leg it from the office right on the 'd' of dot this evening. I've got a sound session to attend which, unusually, is not in nearby Soho (where most sound studios are located) but at the arse end of the Central Line.

I had toyed with the idea of cycling, until Google Maps pointed out that it was over ten miles west, and therefore a twenty-eight mile round trip to get home tonight. Eff that. Especially as I don't want to turn up at the sound session sweating like a BNP candidate on Question Time.

I tube it, instead. It takes forever and almost melts my Oyster card to get there, but I do so in time. I realise straight away why this facility is not in central London. It's fooking massive. By far the biggest I've ever worked in. Unlike its compact Soho counterparts, it is specifically designed for movies. The studio is basically a cinema theatre, but without the seats. And the popcorn. And the sticky carpet. And the person in the row behind asking their other half dumb questions about the plot every few minutes.

It's also the first studio I've been in where there is no separate sound booth for the actors, so the rest of us - the engineers, director, producers and I - must be absolutely silent during takes.

We don't do ADR - additional dialogue recording - in advertising. Well we do, but we don't call it ADR. We call it 'post sync'. Fook knows why it has a different name. But I have now learned how different the approach is to additional recordings in the two industries. In commercials we shoot a thirty-second ad in one to three days. In films we shoot five to seven minutes a day. So, consequently we have the time to shoot far more takes in ads than in films. Which means, in ads, we have far more chances of capturing a performance that doesn't have the rumble of a passing train drowning out a line of dialogue, the hum of a film light breaking the spell of an intimate moment, or the rasp of a crew member snoring during a tense scene*.

ADR is also used to dub in alternative lines where needed. Like for the aeroplane version of the film, for example. The versions of films that are played on aeroplanes don't have swearing in, you see.

This evening we are recording our BLA (brilliant leading actress). So in-demand is she at the moment, filming a TV series and rehearsing for a one-woman play, we are recording with her after-hours. There are quite a few lines to re-record. But also other stuff like breathing, panting, straining, laughing. Needless to say, she nails everything with ease. So the second session we have booked with her in a few evenings won't be needed.

We even re-record the 'fucks' to 'flips' and 'shits' to 'stuffs' for the sensitive ears of the mile high. Despite some complete flipping stuff-for-brains (me) forgetting about the lack-of-separate-sound-booth thing, and noisily helping himself to the biscuits, mid-take.

A cinema without the seats.

* *I swear to you, this actually happened.*

SCORE

YET ANOTHER MORNING to add to my highlights reel of experiences. We've got the composer arriving at the edit house to present his work in progress. It's the second such session we've had with him. The first was great. So the director, editors and I are in high spirits as we scale stepladders to gaffer-tape a sheet of cardboard to the ceiling of the screening room to block out the skylight... To me... to you... to me... to you.

Our score is in accomplished hands. The composer is an Oscar winner. (Sorry, I have already mentioned that. It's just such a fantastic statement to type.) And it's nice to see that being in the pantheon of movie greatness doesn't mean he is above shoving a McMuffin down his neck with the rest of us*.

The score is a really important part of the film. Used well, it leads the viewer through the story, emotionally, without them noticing. It drives the narrative and gives the audience a subtle poke in the ribs at key tender, scary, tense, hopeful and adrenal moments. Much in the same way that a laughter track in a situation comedy tells the viewers when something funny happens. But better. Hopefully.

Music is tricky to get right. Just getting the temporary score sorted for the rough cut, made from music stolen from other films, was a feat. But it formed the basis of the brief to our Oscar winner. From that, he's taken the 'value' of the music in each scene (the emotion we are trying to communicate). Then he's written a theme, a simple melody, that he's been able to play out in different ways depending on the desired emotion of the scene.

In very basic terms, he's written several different versions of the same tune that communicate different emotions. I stress the 'basic terms' mind you. It's far cleverer than that. He's also attached certain melodies and instrumentation to certain characters and situations. So, the appearance of these characters spells danger/tenderness/hope or whatever we need. And being that this is a psychological thriller, he's also distorted, warped and generally fucked with certain tunes and noises to get that 'inside the mind of someone on the edge' feeling that we want.

To achieve it all, he has started from a classical music point of view. But then, to inject the modern psychological stuff, he's used weird homemade instruments and electronic elements. It sounds really complicated, but it isn't to the ear. It's great.

We sit in the screening room, going through each scored scene, one by one. I feel like a right knob whenever I make a comment. I love music, but I am not musical. Two recorder lessons, aged eight, are about the size of my musical training. I am, however SHIT HOT on the dance floor. Seriously, you should have seen me back in eighty-three with my ghetto blaster and roll of lino.

But still, when commissioning music for commercials it's always the bit I feel most challenged by. Not being musically trained means I just don't have the vocabulary. So I express myself by saying things like: 'You know the bit where it goes *wha whhhaa de de de da woooooow?*'

Luckily, as well as not being averse to shoving a filthy breakfast down his neck, the composer is also willing to patiently decipher the ill-informed comments of us non-muso numpties. Not that there is much at all that isn't totally agreeable. We have one more session like this, and then we'll be off to a studio to record it all with a proper orchestra. As I hurry to the office afterwards, I'm humming a tune and my heart is singing.

**It cost me just shy of tenner today.*

***Having said all this, the director and I are fans of a director called Michael Haneke, who never uses music. We adopted his dogmatic approach in the short film version we did and it worked really well, as it goes. We did consider the same approach in the feature for a while, but I'm glad we went down the music route.*

****ING ADR

IT'S THE SUNNIEST DAY of the year. I know, I'll go and spend most of it in a windowless studio in Soho. Oh well, at least I'm in civilisation doing the ADR (additional dialogue record) this time.

We've got so many people coming in to re-record today that the producers have hired a studio in town for the session. Suits me better. As before, we're covering lines of dialogue that have been deemed unusable by our sound designers. There's a lot to do. But it's good to see all the actors again. And they don't seem to mind doing what is quite an involved amount of work.

Our excellent leading male actor throws himself into his performance. Literally. One of the scenes we need him to replicate is a fight scene. But he is really effin impressive. Seriously, every single line he has to re-record, be it an intimate conversation, or a screaming match, he nails one hundred percent faithfully to the filmed original. He is so good; it is verging on the scary.

Another of the talent who comes along is a six year-old child actor. Sorry - six-and-a-half. Fractions are very important at that age. She's come all the way from up t'north for her twenty-minute session, bless her precocious little cotton socks.

For one so young, she says one of the important lines of dialogue in the film. The director and I have argued the toss for weeks about how best it should be delivered in the film. So we decided to get her to re-do it today.

For one so young, she does very well, too. In between pulling the microphone apart and trying to negotiate with her mum that she IS old enough to watch the full film, that is.

The important line is improved, so we let her go to spend the rest of her day in Hamleys. Being a kid, she has no swearing to record clean alternatives of for the 'aeroplane version'. I haven't checked the facts, but I'm assuming the aeroplane version exists because you can't regulate the audience on a plane. Or they don't have a ratings system in the air? I don't know. Whatever, it's taken very seriously. There is actually a published list of forbidden words, with a corresponding list of allowable alternatives beside them. I shit you not. It's sixteen fucking pages of in length, for 'flip' sake. For example...

BASTARD: Blackguard, bozo, butcher, buzzard, buffoon, bad seed, brothers, dullard, beggar, braggart, bum, bimbo, blowhard.

CUNT: Clown, tease, twit, joke, fool, crumb, cat, nag, curse, cheat, couch, cow, crab, dip, crock, creep, wretch, clot, scab, hag.

DICKHEAD: Dumbhead, ditzhead, idiot, dullhead, duntz, butthead, dinkhead, dipso, deadhead, dingbat, dumbbell, fathead, sickhead, dusthead, dirthead, woodhead, hayseed, lummox, ill-breed, dorkhead, pinhead, hothead, blockhead, jughead, lunkhead, saphead, half baked, egghead.

EJACULATE: Eliminate, finish.

HELL: Heck, hey, aww.

PENIS: Person, member, privates, passion, tool, unit, part(s), pelvis, package, putter.

PISSWORM: Tickworm, pinworm, pileworm.

TWAT: Twit.

WANKER: Wacko, weasel, waster, wombat.

There are also three pages of alternatives of all the different versions of 'Fuck' (like fucking hell, fuck around, fuck-face, mother fucker, fuck you, oh fuck, fuck-stick etc). And there's a page and a half of 'shit'. (Shithead, crazy shit, shit hole, shit-storm, shithouse, shit-for-brains, shit-bird, shitload etc.)

Now, being from advertising, where profanity is never allowed, it's not surprising that my non-advertising script is littered with sweariness. It's probably the same reason for the swearing contained in these pages. Cunt! Ah, I can't tell you how liberating that is after writing for a chocolate bar brand all day. Wankers! Cathartic is what it is. Arse-wipe! Or typing Tourette's, depending on how you bastard well look at it.

Anyway, where was I? Yes, I've written the male lead character as a particularly potty-mouthed individual. So we had a lot to re-record with him. My favourite passage being: '*You fucking bitch, get off me. Don't fucking touch me. Fucking bitch, you have fucked it now, you are fucked.*'

Which on an aeroplane will be: '*You stupid cow, get off me. Don't you touch me. Stupid cow, you have done it now, you are finished.*'

Interesting.

Our brilliant second lead actress also had quite a lot. And I argued long and hard, that we didn't have to change her Manc-drawled 'fooks', because 'fook' is not on the list.

I lost; we changed it to 'flip'.

Lucky there's no plane crashes in the film, because there's also a list of visual no-nos. These include plane crashes (fair dos), big explosions/disasters generally, shooting people in the head, the sex act (we've got one of them), dead bodies with their eyes open (got one of them) extreme violence (got a bit of that), injections where you can see the needle penetrating skin, nudity, defecation (err, no, no and no).

So, we'd have to do a re-edit, if it comes to it. I was about to say that I will shudder if this film ever gets played a mile high, but to be honest, that's 'bull talk'. I'll be 'eliminating' in my pants like 'hey' with 'flipping' delight if it ever happens. I'd be a 'dusthead' not to.

And it will mean that when our young actress is flown to Hollywood to star in her next movie, she'll be able to watch herself in the film, after all.

This instalment has been brought to you by the letter F, U, C and effin K. And the number two. Wankers.

SCORE TWO

THIS WORKING-FOR-A-LIVING lark is really getting in the way of my art, daddio. (*Raises back of hand to forehead and sighs.*) Despite the desk fan and the air con on full blast, I am sweating to get a succession of meetings out of the way, so I can join the rest of the gang for another session with the music score composer. Like a schoolboy stuck in a maths lesson until the bell releases him unto his playground football fest, I count down each agonising minute of my various reviews and strategy meetings.

One of the projects I am working on, for a famous brand of chocolate bar, I've been talking about for eight months now and still haven't actually shot the thirty-second commercial.

Jesus, I could have got a feature film away in that time.

Ba-dum-tiss!

But I'm desperate to enjoy as much of the post-production process as I can. As soon as the last meeting finishes, the cycling shoes are on and I'm off to the underground car park where I keep my bike. I 'Froome' it across to North London, laughing in the face of the Highway Code as I go. Ha ha ha.

It's an important session, should I arrive in one piece, because today the composer is taking us through pretty much his finished demo score. So it's not ideal that I am fully three hours late. The meeting is at the studio of our composer's musical collaborator. I love this for two reasons. Firstly, her studio is at Abbey Road (baby). And secondly, her involvement is indicative of a composer who is talented enough not to let his ego get in the way of enlisting the help of others. He has a classical background. But he works with this woman, who is steeped in electronica, when appropriate.

It's cool, but I'm not. I'm hot and breathing heavily as I push into the outer ring (of Regents Park) and pedal like a maniac past Lords cricket ground towards Abbey Road. I'm stopping for nobody. Not the people standing in the middle of the road holding cameras, nor the multitude of Japanese and American tourists that are getting their photos taken as they walk across the famous zebra crossing. Sorry to spoil your photo, guys - the album cover didn't have a blurred image of a bloke zooming past on a bike and nearly flattening Ringo, as far as I can remember.

I turn into the graffiti-strewn entrance and quickly lock up. I rush into the reception where I am met by a pair of startled receptionists. They look at the fat, sweaty, out-of-breath man in front of them as if he is a crazed mentalist Beatles fan about to detonate his backpack. And it doesn't help that, as I attempt to turn on the charm and reassure them that there is no need to press any panic buttons because I'm here legitimately, I instantly forget the name of the person I am here to see.

I try and rescue the situation by phoning the director. But as sweat literally pours out of me like a broken tap, I realise his phone is off, because he is in a sound session. Damn. I take a moment at the water cooler to wet my whistle and attempt to regain my composure. In the meantime, one of the receptionists works out where I need to be and I finally get ushered to the correct studio.

I take my seat in the blissfully air-conditioned room, full of contrition. I've missed bloody loads of it. But I do get a good forty-five minutes of stuff, which is better than nothing. I am, however, a bit like a footballer that comes on for the last three minutes of a football match just to get his appearance money. I never really get into to the pace of it and my contribution is not worth the money. Not that I am actually getting paid*.

Anyway, it all sounds brilliant to my ears. Everyone else is happy, too. And it was good to be here for some of it, and get to meet the composer's collaborator and hang out at Abbey Road Studios (baby).

The director has been bringing his fifteen year-old son to these sessions, too. He's a nice lad (like his old man) and very musically talented (unlike his old man). In fact, he is getting a credit for a piece of incidental music that he composed for the film. There's a scene where the two lead characters are in a car. I wrote it that 'loud drum and bass music plays' as they drive along. Now, you know how difficult and expensive it is to license a recognised track, don't you. So the director got his boy to knock us something up in his bedroom, instead. And you know what? It's spot on. And annoyingly catchy. Nobody on set could get the tune, and the repeated sample of a Jamaican accented 'Eaaaaasy Bubba', out of their heads for days afterwards.

Job done, except that the director had to insist that the track is entitled 'Easy Bubba', rather than his son's preferred choice of 'Pussyhole Thief'.

Sorry lad, but as a creative person you're going to have to get used to compromise, I'm afraid.

** A writer's paid involvement in a feature film ends on the first day of the shoot.*

ORCHESTRAL MANOEUVRES IN CHISWICK PARK

THE MCMUFFIN TRADITION goes right out of the window today. There are thirty-odd people coming to the score recording session and I'm not made of money. Anyway, I'm way off the plot out here on the westerly tendrils of the District Line. I haven't got a clue where the nearest purveyor of breakfast filth resides. So an M&S Fruit Salad scoffed on the tube it is, then.

As I stroll towards the studio, full of passion (-fruit, mango, pineapple, etc.) guided by my smartphone, I take in the beautiful Palladian terraces and the whiff of toasted barley emanating from the Fullers brewery, nearby. I also take in the hum of traffic from the adjacent A4, which must easily knock thirty percent from the value of said beautiful Palladian terraces.

I find the studio, just about. Its doorway takes the word 'inconspicuous' to another level. Not only does it not have a sign, it doesn't even have a number. But once inside, it is as lavish and cutting-edge a recording edifice as any I've been in. It turns out it is owned by the frontman of one of the world's biggest eighties rock bands. Which explains the lack of livery out front – it isn't run as a commercial enterprise – and gives an insight into just how much money for nothin' the owner made back in the day. Definitely worth a blister, or two, on his little finger or maybe on his thumb.

I greet the various engineers, all of whom look far too young to be doing what they're doing, with handshakes. I man-hug the composer, the producer and production photographer. I air-kiss the assistant producer. I fist-bump the director and director's son. Then sit down for a rest.

The day is to be split into three. First in, is a solo guitarist. Although, if it wasn't for the guitar case and amp in his hands, I'd have thought he was here to fix the photocopier. Rock 'n' roll he is not. He's a jazz guitarist. Then again, whatever jazz guitarists look like, he doesn't look like one of them, either. And to compound the not judging books by their covers, he then proceeds to inform me that the amp he's clutching isn't an amp, it's every amp in the world*. WTF?! I am still reeling from this as the composer hands the guitarist some sheet music and he starts to play.

The way it works today is each musical part of the film is treated like an individual track in an album. We already have the electronic elements of each piece, so the musicians play the live parts along to the recorded elements with the help of a metronome clicking out the time, err, metronomic-ally. In addition, the corresponding film scene is played on screens around the studio, so the composer and the rest of us can see if it's working to picture.

Jesus, the guitarist is good. Each take is beautiful. It has a jazz infused improvised feel, even though it's played note for note from the sheet music. Hearing an instrument part isolated like this is really pleasing – I remark that we should just use the guitar alone and forget the rest of the instruments, only half jokingly. But it's also difficult to judge. However, the composer gives him the odd word of direction. The director even chips in with a 'perhaps this part can be more hopeful?' now and again. And the guitarist is able to play exactly the same piece, but with a slightly different emotional feel. It's very impressive stuff. I feel extremely privileged to be a part of it, albeit as an onlooker.

With all the guitar parts in the can, and our maestro packing up his kit, I chat to him about his enviable job. He explains that he splits his time between session work, composing for the screen, and recording and performing in his own jazz quartet. He even points me in the direction of his CD release on Amazon, one of which is now on order. Cool, daddio.

We repair to the nearest restaurant for a quick lunch – a Greek taverner complete with dodgy frescos on the walls, plastic vine leaves overhead, and a tiled roof above the bar. I say quick, it doesn't turn out to be. On a day of meeting very talented people, the waiter is well up there. For in this otherwise empty Grecian establishment, he is also the drinks pourer, the maître d and the chef. There are eight of us and we've all asked for different dishes. It's a tall order, but he is equal to it.

The humus is excellent. I know, because I have very good sense of humus. And the main courses are much more evocative of the Aegean than expected once they arrive. But we have to hurry our man up with the bill, somewhat, when we start observing a trickle of people shuffling past the restaurant in the direction of the studio, lugging instrument cases. This afternoon we are recording a twenty-six-string orchestra. (The producers obviously negotiated the composer down from forty strings.) And no matter how heartrending our story is about our poor waiter, they won't get the violins out for us if we're late.

It's comforting to know that if there's a problem printing off the sheet music, there's someone to fix the copier.

* *It's not until after the session that it is explained that every make and model of amp has its own unique sound. This digital box can synthesise the sound of any amp ever made. So our man can create the feel of a Muddy Waters or a Johnny Marr with the twist of a dial. Impressive. I bet Muddy couldn't change the toner on a Xerox 7725.*

ORCHESTRAL MANOEUVRES IN CHISWICK PARK, PART TWO

I'VE SEEN MY TEAM WIN at Wembley. I've samba-d at The Maracana. I've leapt in the mosh pit of Brixton Academy. Sat front and centre at Ronnie Scott's. Seen a world record at the Olympics. I've walked through Deptford alone at night. Only last weekend, at a wedding in a 13th Century church, I heard the Lords prayer sung by a chorister in Aramaic. What I'm saying is, the hairs on the back of my neck are well used to standing on end. But sitting on a DFS three-seater in front of a twenty-six-string orchestra belting out music composed specifically for a film that I have written, pretty much tops the lot. In non-alcohol assisted terms, anyway.

We return from our Grecian interlude. From the control room, we watch the orchestra getting their shit together on the other side of the triple-glazed floor-to-ceiling glass wall. They are a motley crew, are the orchestra (not Motley Crew). The youngest looks about twenty-three and funky. The oldest practically hobbles in on a Zimmer frame; he's so bloody ancient.

Some of them look like housewives. Housewives with violins. And they are dressed not in eveningwear, as expected, but in normal civvies appropriate for these balmy summer temperatures. Hang on; classical orchestras always wear evening dress, don't they? Even The Muppets. I mean, Jesus. I might as well be looking at the contents of a doctor's waiting room, not a roomful of musical prodigies.

Sartorial disappointments aside, when the engineer presses the button that allows us to hear what's going on in there, the pre-performance cacophony of chatter and discordant bow stroke fills the room with the same expectant buzz of excitement as you'd get when taking your seat at the Albert Hall. It does me, anyway.

The composer doesn't seem excited. He carries on like it's a normal day at the office. Which, for him, it is. He wanders through to the studio and the director and I shuffle in behind him, as surreptitiously as we can. As we enter, the orchestra falls into a hushed silence, which I assume is in reverence to the composer rather than suspicion of the interlopers in his wake. While the two non-musos perch on a leather sofa, the composer explains the story of the film to the musicians. He does a good job. They lap it up. He wanders off back to the control room, but we stay. The conductor takes to the lectern. There's a bit of chatter between him and the composer in his earpiece. And one of the orchestra, a female violinist, starts piping up with some comments, too. There's always one.

Finally settled, the conductor waves his baton, and they're off. To describe the next few minutes of experiencing the first take of the opening piece of music in the film, without being wanky, is impossible. So apologies for saying it's an absolutely amazing, intense, surreal and satisfying moment. Beautiful. But spoiled slightly by the mouthy violinist. Here she goes again: 'Can we have the playback in the cans down a little, the lead-in slightly longer, the lights in the studio turned up and the air-con turned down?'

Jesus, who let her in? I lean over to my mate and wonder out loud if a twenty-five-string orchestra would be better, but he explains that she is the First Violin. And as such, she is basically the foreman of the orchestra who speaks on their behalf to the conductor. Oh, right. As you were, love.

After a few more glorious takes, the director and I slip back to the control room. Here, we can hear the strings in context of the other recorded elements (the electronica, the piano, the guitar) and watch it against picture. And it is here that I make my one and only contribution of the day. I suggest that one of the musical cues happen slightly later, and it is agreed that it is, indeed, a good idea. Flushed with success, I attempt to tune in to the composer and conductor conversations between takes. But they speak in some unintelligible musical language that means eff all to me. It tickles me so much how Greek it is that I record the conversation on my phone. Here is a sample verbatim...

'...In thirty-three, have a tiny little crescendo and de-crescendo, then bar thirty-four is just a crotchet, but do be a little bit bolder with the hairpins to make it warmer. And let's all do the same at A, adjusting dynamics below, slightly. And could you put a quaver rest at the end of thirty-five, please?

A quaver rest? We're only just back from lunch.

After spending the rest of the afternoon alternating between sitting in the studio and the control room, enraptured, I hear the orchestra's denouement. It's been so interesting to witness them with their strange dialect, their own little culture of heavenly note-perfect performance, interspersed with gossip and easy laughter. They are a very nice bunch of people.

As soon as they clear the studio, a bloke arrives to fit a new carpet. At least I assume that's what he's here for until the composer tells me he's one of the finest solo cellists in the business. Let me tell you, if he is even half as good with a roll of Axminster as he is with a cello, he would definitely get wall-to-wall bookings.

Not a dickie bow or ball gown in sight.

The cellist on a mid-grey, twill-pile, wool-mix rug.

WHITE MAN IN HAMMERSMITH MALAISE*

IT'S THE MUSIC MIX this evening. It's in Chiswick again. My office is at Russell Square. It's a balmy evening. Shall I get the tube and arrive a bit sweaty, or the quicker option of cycling the seven miles but turning up looking like I've taken a shortcut through a car wash?

This dilemma is solved for me when I get an e-mail saying the session has been brought forward an hour and I am, therefore, already late. So I leave work so prompt and early I share the lift to G with the secretaries. I jump astride my aluminium steed and pedal like the effin clappers. I whizz down to Holborn and swing a right, interpreting the Highway Code as creatively as safety will allow. Man, I've forgotten what a shitehouse of a road Oxford Street is. What with the potholes, the pedestrians leaping off the curbs like lemmings, the traffic lights every fifty yards and the BWAs (Bus drivers with attitude) it's a wonder I make it to the other side of Marble Arch without incident.

I love cycling in London, don't get me wrong. It's exciting and liberating. Adrenal even. And it allows me to enjoy the city's sights much more than I would if I were stuck on the tube every day. But no matter how carefully I ride I have at least one near miss on every journey. And no matter how much I pedal like my life depends on it (which, I suppose, it does) pretending I am Mark Cavendish (I'm not rakish enough to pretend I'm Bradley Wiggins), there are always quicker riders on the road to remind me of my advanced age and receded athleticism.

Tonight it's a bloke overtaking me on the downhill stretch between Holland Park and Shepherds Bush who does it. He bombs past me on one of those sandwich delivery bikes, for fuck sake. I catch up and steal a jump on him at the next lights that he can't respond to. But it's not a real victory. He did me. I know it and he knows it. Oh well, getting beaten by a professional cyclist isn't the end of the world. (He rides that bloody sandwich bike for a living, so that counts as a professional cyclist in my book.) But I will NEVER let myself be bested by someone on a Barclays bike.

A man must have some pride. Even if it does come before a fall. Mine being the moment I overtake a Barclays biker on the Hammersmith gyratory and my back tyre turns into a pancake. I've always hated the bloody Hammersmith gyratory. Balls. I'm about two miles away from the studio with a puncture. I ask a couple of people if there is a bike shop in the area. No one seems to know. Even Google is not much help. So I take my chances in a pound shop. The shopkeeper won't let me in the cramped Aladdin's cave of an establishment with my bike. So I have to wait a couple of minutes for the custom to die down before he fetches me one, himself. I applaud the personal service, but not the price. One ninety-nine for a repair kit in a pound shop is taking the oxymoronic piss. But this pound shop is like an ice-cream van parked outside Madame Tussauds to me right now – they can charge whatever they like.

I cough up and stride on. I calculate that it is marginally quicker to walk to Chiswick from here, than to try and repair the wheel at the side of the road, then ride. It still takes forever. And by the time I buzz the inconspicuous door and enter the blissfully air conditioned studio, I've missed virtually the whole session. I literally get to hear the mix of the final scene, is all. Which, when added to the two minutes of ribbing I take on the sweaty chin from everyone, adds up to precisely five minutes of studio time. And that's it, the sound session is over.

The producer offers to buy me a pint to cheer me up, which I appreciate, but politely decline. All I want to do is fix my bike and go home. And fair play to the director, despite ripping the piss right out of me, he does help me fix the puncture**.

What a waste of an evening that was.

'Oh well, just chalk it off as one of those things' I tell myself as I start pedalling the fourteen miles home. But then a bloke on a Brompton foldy-uppy overtakes me on Chelsea Embankment and the red mist descends.

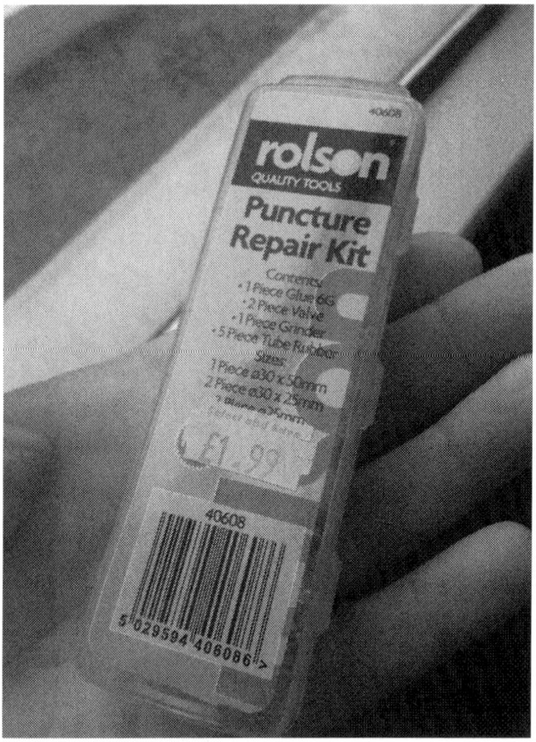

They saw me coming.

** I can't tell you how pleased I am with this pun.*

***The director did a solo ride from Land's End to John O'Groats a couple of years back, so is expert in roadside puncture repairs. And Premier Inns.*

GRADE

WE'VE MADE THE GRADE. Well chuffed. It has been two months since we locked the edit down. Plus two and a half months of editing time before then. Which, all in all, adds up to a long time looking at a rough picture.

Now, I'm aware that anyone reading this without filmmaking experience doesn't really know what I'm on about. Colour grading is the process of altering and enhancing the colour of the film. It's like when you take a photo on your smartphone and then put it through a filter on Instagram. That's a colour grade. And when applied to a film, it transforms it from looking like an episode of The Bill, to something altogether more filmic, like Die Hard. If it were a cop movie, that is. (It isn't.)

Grading is always a brilliant moment. You're so used to it looking like The Bill, that when it suddenly starts looking like Die Hard, it really lifts your spirits.

Grade sessions are also a great doss. In commercials, the writer basically sits in a darkened room all day sending out for expensive coffee and sushi, while the operator (they call themselves 'colourists') works their magic. Art directors (the other half of the advertising creative team duo) and directors, often get quite juiced up about 'crushing the blacks', 'dialling up the magentas' and 'warming the skin tones' etc. But in general it's a nice day out of the office. An ad is typically one day of grading, but our film is eight. There are over one hundred and eighty times more pictures to grade, but only eight times more grading time. That just shows you how much more indulgent commercials are. In those eight days I'll dip in and out when I can - lunchtimes, evenings.

Today, however, I eschew the baked potato from the local Italian cafe (#SupportIndependentTraders) and cycle to Soho for a little lunchtime peek. And if I get a cheeky deluxe sashimi box with edamame and miso soup out of it, too, then who am I to complain? But, no. When I arrive I am told that everyone is out on their lunch break. What? You mean you don't work through lunch and order from a swanky restaurant? How annoyingly un-indulgent is that?

That's the second time my advertising indulgent-ness has been exposed in this suite, goddammit. Back in January during pre-production, the director and director of photography had just shot a camera test at our prime location. We were here to view the footage on the big screen in order to decide whether to shoot on film or digital. When the runner came in to take a drinks order, and I asked for a beer, all the film people laughed and said 'spot the bloke in advertising'. Bloody hell, It was only a beer, not a gram of powder and a stripper to snort it off.

Anyway, it's just as well that the suite is empty, because some guys are here to interview the director and I. They are from a film festival that we won awards at with our short film last year. It was the success of the short that got us to make the feature, so we're really happy to help*. But we didn't expect them to want to film us.

Blimey. The best I can hope for is to not come over like a complete idiot. It's a big ask, what with my tied tongue and sweaty brow.

Luckily, the interview is cut short by everyone returning from lunch. Phew. We agree that the rest of the questions will be answered via e-mail, and I assure them that I will be far more articulate in writing. And before I have to dash back to the office, I get an enjoyable half an hour of seeing Reg Hollis transformed into Bruce Willis.

* *To begin, we had no luck attracting funding for the feature film. So we shot an abridged first act as a short /trailer for the feature. It worked, and less than a year later, here I am in the grade session. Mental. So I can highly recommend making a short as a way of getting to make a feature film.*

GRADE TWO

I ARRIVE AT THE POST HOUSE in Soho with a quintet of delicious breakfast filth about my personage. I'm looking forward to this morning's session. We're going to be watching the whole film, in order to review the graded pictures. I haven't watched the film for ages. It's been odd making such a long-form piece of work, after so many years of thirty-second time-lengths. Once the edit's locked, all the other elements - like the sound, music, visual effects – have been looked at, scene by scene. So it's been a challenge to retain perspective. Particularly when the only other viewing we've had recently (for the music) I was punctured out of.

As I enter the suite and distribute the McMuffins, the operator (the dude doing the grade) is surprised by this culinary generosity. I explain to him that this ritual is a golden arch-shaped rod that I have made for my own back. Rooted in my acute awareness of how lucky I am, as a writer, to be allowed into the post-production phase. He nods. It's a kind of knowing nod. One that says: 'Oh, I get you. You're part of the culture of using food as a reward and symbol of affection, thereby associating food that is fundamentally bad, with happiness and love, fuelling both the profits of the evil multinational corporations and the obesity levels of the western world in equal sickening measure. You bastard.'

But then he says "Nice one, thanks mate." and starts eating it, gleefully, so I think I probably misread the nod, to be fair.

Anyway, the suite is fandabidozy. It's basically a cinema, but with an equipment desk at the back and one row of eight seats in front of a screen that fills the entire front wall. When I say seats, they are like business class airline seats, complete with acres of cowhide and buttons to make them go from upright, all the way to horizontal. The director and I immediately start messing about with the buttons like a couple of five-year-olds in Land of Leather. But it's nigh on impossible to drink your coffee in a horizontal seat, so I put it back to a sensible position as the countdown clock on the screen leads us to the opening shot of the film.

It's ~~good~~ fucking ace to watch the graded pictures. They look incredible next to the off-line picture. And it's worthwhile to watch it all 'on the run' like this, rather than odd scenes in isolation, because it's easier to notice stuff that need attention.

We don't watch it in one hit, however. There are five rolls of film that make up the film in its entirety. Each one is about twenty minutes in length. So we view it one reel at a time. Even so, we have to take notes every time we spot something that needs finessing, as it's easy to forget in that time.

On the first reel, one thing that sticks out like a dogs doodah, is the sky in one of the scenes. Jesus, the bad continuity weather has come back to haunt me again five months later*.

But in general, it looks bloody brilliant. The operator has done a fantastic job. And for the first time, the benefits of shooting on 35mm film are shining through. There's richness to everything.

The depths of field are more defined. And in the close-ups, you can read every bit of emotion in the actors' eyes. The director remarks that it has somehow made their performances even stronger. I am in full agreement. The tone of the pictures is definitely adding an extra layer of mood and meaning to the whole thing.

God, this film is coming together, it's really coming together. I could watch this all day long, man. But just as we're about to start reel five, I get an e-mail from work saying my afternoon meeting has been moved forward, and is now starting in twenty minutes. So I have to pedal like a lunatic to get back in time. One's work comes before one's hobby, I'm afraid. Even if it is the best effin hobby in the world.

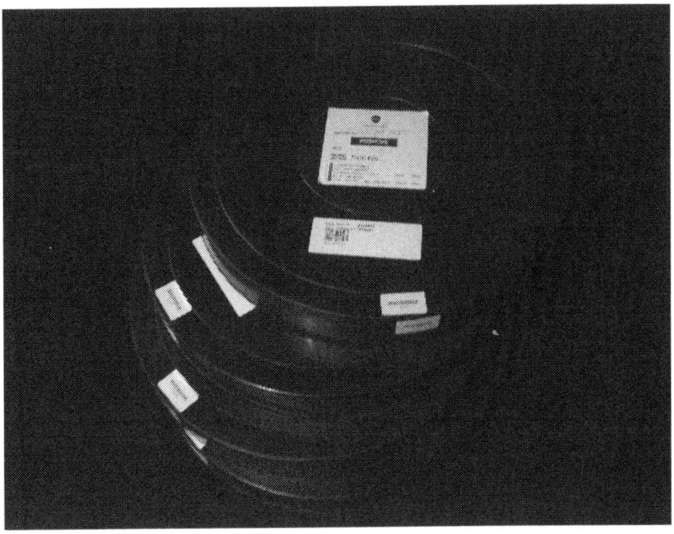

Four of the five rolls of film that are the film.

* *On the first day of the shoot my sweary quote about the weather messing our continuity up, was printed on a leading*

national entertainment magazine's website. Read all about it in 'PR Disaster'.

FINAL PICTURE

IT'S OUR LAST VISIT to the grade today. It's going to be another goody sitting in our business class seats, despite the lack of airhostesses serving champagne. It's a review session, is this. So we'll be watching and signing off on the finished picture. This includes the grade, but also all the VFX work and titling, too. I am conscious that I haven't really touched on these elements of the post-production process, thus far. The reason for that is I haven't had much involvement in them. 'But you've had very little involvement in any of it, from what we've read.' I hear you cry.

'Well, eff you.' I retort in probably the world's first imagined argument between a writer and his reader(s). Anyway, let's just calm down, we're too mature for this. 'Well, we are' I hear you say.

'Okay, okay, you win.' I reply, holding my hands up in defeat then returning them to the keyboard to plough on, regardless of the imaginary heckling.

No, unlike in commercials where VFX (visual effects) sessions are considered another opportunity for time out of the office, ordering thirty-two types of exquisite raw fish, we don't hang out in the suite. Maybe we would if it was a heavy post job. Like a film with a load of specky kids flying around on broomsticks, or something. But all the things on our VFX list are quite matter-of-fact jobs that can be approved over e-mail. (And the director popping in from time to time.) We're talking changing a car number plate, painting out a cable that shouldn't be there, removing an Uncle Buck-esque mole from someone's face. That sort of thing.

Even the one and only stunt we have in the film is a fairly straightforward green-screen number*. Well, straightforward by the standards of our excellent VFX guys, anyway.

The job of designing the titles has been given to the director's mate. Sounds like nepotism, but it's far from it. His mate happens to own one of the foremost graphic design practices. He's a serious design hombre. A design don, even. He is so high up in the design world, in fact, that he does the graphic design work for the Design Museum. So there are no complaints from me. Besides, he'd already designed us a really cool opening sequence for our short film. Having said that, this is a slightly different kettle of fish. Rather than a standalone title sequence, we want the opening titles to appear over the beginning of the film this time.

The response is simple and elegant. Just as Miles Davis believed the notes that you don't play are the most important, there is nothing over-egged about the titles.

Nothing flash, or too 'designed', just a distinctive way of setting the type that can also be applied to the closing credits, promotional material around the film (posters etc.) and the rollers (the rolling titles at the end of the film). And he spelt my name correctly, which is good. But I notice that he didn't set my name bigger, bolder and up for longer than all the other credits, like I asked him to.

As the rollers creep up the screen at the end of the review session, approved, it means we now have a finished picture. Hoorah. All we need to do is the sound mix now.

** 'Green screen' is the technique of filming actors in front of a green background. (It used to always be a blue background, but it changed to green. Don't ask me why.) This allows the VFX guys to strip in any background they like, be it separately shot live action, or computer generated monsters or whatever.*

SOUND MIX

DON'T GET ME WRONG, I'm not a Perivale-ist. Some of my best mates come from Perivale*. But I actually do hate the place. Most sound studios are in Soho, which is only a few pedal strokes from my office. But the one we're using is in zone thirty-seven on the Central Line. I can't just wander away from my desk 'for a coffee' and join the session for a bit when I have an opportune moment. No, getting to Perivale is a military exercise of meeting rescheduling and late night working to catch up on missed office time. It takes about forty minutes to get there. Longer if you get on the train destined for the wrong branch of the line and have to get off and go back a couple of stops to get on the right one. But you'd have to be a complete numpty to do that. (Or a film director.)

We did much of the ADR (additional dialogue recording) in Perivale last month and it's where we're now doing the final sound mix (also known as the dub). The sound mix is when all the aural elements of the film are brought together and mixed into one coherent soundtrack. The elements being: the field recordings (the sound recorded on the shoot), the ADR, the Foley** (sound added in post production) and the composed music score.

The sound mix is the final piece in the jigsaw of the filmmaking process. So it's very exciting. This excitement is dampened somewhat as I step off the tube at Perivale at the precise moment it decides to bucket down with rain. (We're so far out, even The Underground is above ground in Perivale.) So I have to leg it the, thankfully, small distance to the studio.

Despite the close proximity, I am soaked by the time I fall in the revolving door and introduce myself to the receptionist. She finds it hilarious. What? Have you never seen an out-of-breath soaking-wet middle-aged grey-haired man wearing headphones and steamed-up glasses before, love?

The runner smirks, too, as he shows me to the vast sound suite. Of course, once inside, the benefit of the studio's location is reaped. The suite is fucking enormous. It has a humungous screen and a gargantuan desk of sound equipment that needs three men to operate. (You get one sound engineer in a commercial dub.) As per effing usual, I am late. And I walk in just as they're looking at a complicated scene, sound-wise, that has atmos, music and dialogue in. It sounds like a complete mess to me. And I say as much. I'm not saying anything they don't know. A bit of the problem is, we're used to the temporary sound, so suddenly applying all our new shiny elements makes it all a bit much and changes the whole tone of the scene. But these guys are on it. I love working with sound engineers like these. They are the types who are always concentrating hard on what they're doing, but still have half an ear to the room to hear our reactions and opinions. So while the director, producer and I are busy thinking out loud and discussing the issues, they are responding to and solving the problems before we even get around to ask them to.

Basically, they are 'on it',. And it's great to hear our composed music and clean dialogue next to our luscious graded pictures.

Like the grade, there is over a week in the schedule for the mix. Like the grade, I'll be popping across when I can and making sure I am around for the reviews. Well, I say popping across. I'll be writing off a whole afternoon, then going back to the office and working until stupid o'clock to make up for it, when I can.

Bloody Perivale.

** I made that up. I don't actually know anyone who lives in this cultural desert.*

*** Foley is all the added sounds that haven't been captured on the shoot (or ones that need to be replaced). It can be anything. The sound of someone getting punched in the face, a door closing, footsteps, wind. I've had loads of fun doing Foley for TV and radio commercials down the years and would have liked to have joined-in with the film Foley, but they just got on with it themselves. As well as a lot of in-studio recordings, they also went back to a lot of the locations we shot at to record atmos. Yes, they took it very seriously, indeed.*

It's called Foley after the bloke who pioneered it in Hollywood back when the 'talkies' first started being made. Not after Eddie Murphy's character in the hit film, Beverley Hills Cop, you understand. (Get the fuck outta here!)

FINISHED FILM / HALFWAY POINT

I DON'T CARE HOW BUSY I AM at work, there's no way on this ungodly earth am I going to give today's session a swerve. No way. No way. No way, do you hear me? It's the final review of the final mix of the film. Not being there would be like missing the birth of your own child, or something.

It starts at two p.m. So I get to the office before nine - which is early for me - with the intention of having a full and productive morning. As I stroll in, in my dripping-wet cycling attire and head to the café area to make myself a cuppa, I notice that there's loads of breakfast stuff laid out. Toast, cereal - the lot. Apparently, there's free breakfast for staff here every morning before nine. How civilised is that? Shame I'm not a morning person. This is a staff benefit I rarely enjoy. And as I munch my Marmite on toast at my desk, still in my smelly cycling gear, I need to mess around on Facebook for a while before I can gain enough momentum to click open the Word document I am creating a multi-award-winning advertising idea upon*.

This week, I am working on an ad campaign on behalf of a government department. After I've cooled down, I have a shower (to my colleagues' relief) and way before ten, I am, headphones on, and right in the zone. So much so that the next time I look at the clock, it's past the time I should be leaving for effin Perivale. I unplug my headphones from my laptop, stick it in my phone and run for the tube.

By the time I get to P-vale (I bet the local youth call it that to make it sound ghetto) I realise that, in my haste, I hadn't picked up any lunch. Shit! Places like Prêt a Manger don't seem to exist out here, and I haven't got time to go walking around the area blindly looking for a sandwich shop. (Besides, I don't want to run the risk of getting jacked by the P-vale Massive, man.) It's two 'o'clock now. I can't go beyond four p.m. on two bits of toast. Like it or not, it's going to have to be a chicken tikka sandwich and lamb samosa from the newsagent at the tube station.

I daren't look at the 'use by' dates on the packaging as I unwrap my pungent luncheon in the studio. And I purposefully sit right at the back of the room, well away from the three engineers, two producers, director and son of director, who are also present.

It doesn't matter where I sit, because the screen is immense. I take a photo of it, but because there's no context, you can't tell how big it is in the photo. So the director takes one of me standing in front of the screen for scale. Then, dicking about over with, we settle down to watch our final review. This time we are going to watch it from beginning to end without interruption, just like a punter hopefully will at the pictures. It's a wonderful feeling to watch it with all the elements finally in place.

For the first time, I pretty much watch the thing just as a viewer, rather than with a critical eye. I take the odd note. But nothing major. And as the last scene fades, the final score fills the darkened room and the credits roll, (I can't believe I'm admitting this) I get a bit dewy-eyed and lumpy throated. Soppy sod.

I do compose myself when the lights go up, though. And we chat through the few issues we want to look at for the final time.

It takes twenty minutes of fiddling, and we're done. We shake hands. The director admits that he is absolutely exhausted. All the pressure of the year is suddenly off. And now he's at the finish line, he's knackered. I am a bit, too.

It feels odd. And it's not just the samosa repeating on me. It's a little anti-climactic, if I'm honest. The head sound guy proclaims that he has the company credit card to buy us a few celebratory drinks. We would all love to. Apart from everything else, it's four p.m. on a summer Friday, so we should definitely be hanging out of a pub somewhere. But no, I have to go back to catch up on the afternoon of work I've just missed, one of the producers has her wedding arrangements to sort out, and the director has a storyboard to work on for a commercial he's doing. Jesus, the director and I weren't expecting to complete the film and then jump in the limo straight to the Leicester Square premier, but we thought we'd get to celebrate it a bit more than a fist-bump on the platform at pissing P-vale tube station.

I suppose it's because this isn't actually the end. Getting a finished product is actually the halfway point of the process. We've now got to sell our product to distributers in order to get a theatrical release. I know, mental. The next few months are going to be very interesting. Or boring, or tough, or exciting, or excruciating. Or a combination of all of them. Christ knows. But I tell you what; I'll let you know...

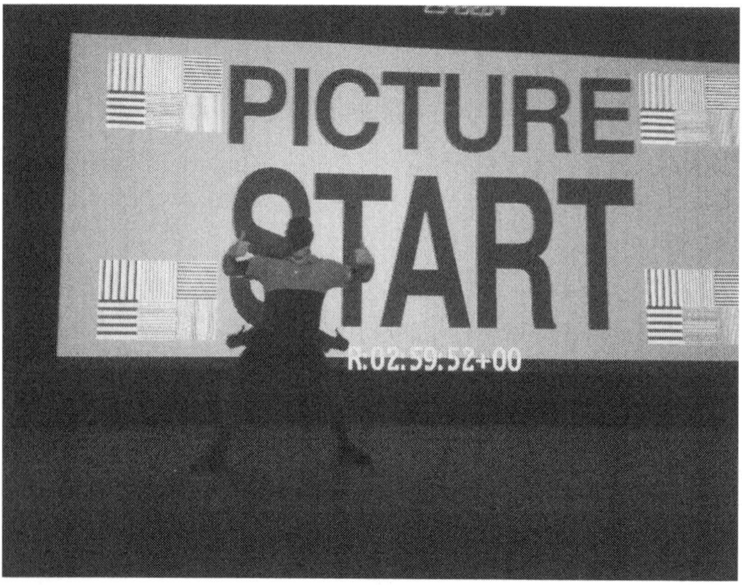

Out the way! We're trying to watch a movie!

* *All creative people must believe, with at least a tiny bit of conviction, that the project they are working on is going to be brilliant, is going to get made, is going to transform the fortunes of the brand they are promoting and win a shitload of awards around the world. Thus putting noughts on their salary and gaining the respect, adulation and jealousy of their peers. We have to suspend disbelief in this way to not let the fact that upwards of ninety-five percent of our work never happens, dampen our creative enthusiasm and will to live.*

As Churchill said, the definition of success is the ability to go from one failure to the next with no loss of enthusiasm. Too right Winnie. If me and my director mate had let our seven years of getting nowhere with our film projects grind us down, we would never have got this movie in the can, and I wouldn't be sitting here spouting all this self-indulgent twaddle.

Then again, Einstein said that the definition of insanity was doing the same thing over and over again and expecting a different result. So without disagreeing with either of those two Colossi, I suppose you could say it takes some kind of insane optimism to be a creative person. And miserableness, of course.

PART FOUR
PRE-RELEASE

PMT (POST MOVIE TENSION)

SO, HOW'S THE FILM GOING? - Say all my friends, family, colleagues, acquaintances and pretty much anyone I have a conversation with at the mo.

"Yeah. Good. We finished it a few days back". I retort, trying not to sound too showy-offy (but failing).

"What, the whole thing?" They reply, "The sound, music, titles, and everything else?"

"Yeah. Everything. I can't quite believe it."

"Brilliant" they all say. Then follow it with: "So what next?"

That's the bit where the conversation starts to falter. I know that we need to get a distribution deal. But I don't know for certain quite how we're going to get one.

This takes people aback a little. I think they think we make the film for a planned release date. That in a couple of weeks they'll be able to go and see it at their local multiplex, munching on a bucket of overpriced popcorn and a two litre carton of Coke. Maybe a little box of Poppets. That would be nice. But they don't realise that, in independent film, there is no release date.

We are about half way in the process, in truth. We now need to go out with our finished film and find more investment for its release. This is because no film, however fantastic, will ever get put on at even one cinema for one day unless there is a budget for its promotion. We're talking film posters, press ads, a theatrical trailer, TV, radio and cinema ads, and screenings to film critics. All these things are vital and need to be in place before you can get it on at the cinema. This can add up to nearly as much as is spent making the film itself. So if anyone is ever going to see the film, we need to get a deal with a distributer*.

"That's crazy" the people say, "you've essentially just made a very expensive product without a shop to sell it in."

"'Yes, crazy." I agree. Then say that this is how independent film works. And that obviously, the producers who have invested in the creative product - which is the script and the director - have a lot of experience in knowing what constitutes a project with a realisable commercial potential.

"So, how do you get a distributer?" is the next question.

"Oh, I don't fucking know, get off my back, I'm just the writer. Jesus!" I want to say, but don't.

"Err, I think we need to get a sales agent next, or enter it into film festivals. I'm not quite sure" is more along the lines of what I do say.

Actually, I think we need to get both. A sales agent is an intermediary who will take on the film and act as the negotiator with the distributer. So we need to get one of those and enter the film into one of the major film festivals** at the same time. So by the time the festival comes around, we have a sales agent in place to flog the film around the world***.

Of course, the other thing about getting a film into one of the major festivals is the exposure you get to critics. Gaining a 'festival buzz' around your film ahead of the release can really help it find a large audience.

Take Michael Haneke's, Amour; a subtitled French film about two old people dying. I doubt that anyone in this country would have even known about it if it weren't for the buzz of winning the Palm D'or at the Cannes Film Festival.

Another example of this is happening right now. And the film is of special interest to me, as the editor of it is also one of the two editors on our film. What's more, the director is a guy from a commercials background and the writer is an advertising copywriter like myself. He's the most awarded ad copywriter in the business, in fact. His most well known ad (directed by the bloke he's collaborating with on the film) is one for black alcohol involving surfers and horses. But sod it. I bet I'm a better footballer than him. And I suppose, as he is the only other person I can think of who has done the copywriter/screenwriter balancing act, it puts me in very auspicious company.

Anyway, their film has just been premiered at The Venice Biennale. It is the director's third film and it stars an internationally famous Hollywood actress. (It's my director's first film and it stars a nationally famous brilliant British actress.) And it has gone down an absolute storm. Critics either love it or absolutely hate it. I'm serious. The Independent gave it one star but the Guardian gave it five! One critic in Variety magazine slated it, but another critic in Variety raved about it and even slagged his colleague off for his negativity. And I don't know what The Mail Online thought of the film, but they printed twenty pictures of the actress in her low cut dress on the red carpet. You can even see my mate, the editor, sat behind her grinning like a Cheshire cat in one of them. So Marmite-esque are the reviews, film fans will HAVE TO go to the cinema and decide for themselves. A really great position to be in. I for one can't wait to see it. But despite the buzz, this film hasn't yet had a general release date announced.

It a slow old process.

"Yeah, but how you gonna get a sales agent?"

Bloody hell, they don't let up.

The next thing we need to do is put on a screening to some select industry people where we show them the finished film. And to demonstrate that we have a marketable product for them to sell, we need to show them some mock-ups of film posters and other advertising material we have.

Sigh. A copywriter/screenwriter's work is never done.

** The distributer is the company that takes the responsibility of the marketing of the film. They may own the cinemas too. Or they may not. But as experts in bums-on-seats they are the ones that decide when and where your film is released to make money back through ticket sales. They get paid before the production company, of course****.*

*** There are four major film festivals around the world that are also international sales conferences. These are Cannes, Berlin, Toronto and Venice. So getting one of those laurel leaf logos on your poster gives you a good chance of getting your film released* *around the world, because all the international distributers would have seen it****.*

**** Getting a film released in your own country is one thing. But getting it sold around the world is important, as it is how many independent films see a profit****.*

***** Take all the factual information I'm giving you with a pinch of salt, as I am no authority on any of it. No, when this stuff actually starts happening, I'll be able to fill you in properly. But until then, I'm just a shit Wikipedia, really.*

PAN AND SCAN (AND A TOSSER IN A VAN)

THE LAST WEEK AT WORK before a holiday is always excruciating. You are so close to the finish line, you can almost taste the sangria (or whatever the local tipple is where you're going). So a week of fourteen-hour days has been a bitch. I get to Friday pretty frazzled and thinking it was a mistake to book a Friday evening flight rather than a Saturday morning one. The plan is to get to work early for the free-before-nine office breakfast. Do some meetings. Then stop by the 'Pan and Scan' session in Soho at lunchtime, before getting home to pack my suitcase and do the last office meeting of the day via conference call. Simples.

The first bit goes to plan. So I'm loving life as I swing by the 'Pan and Scan' session. No, I didn't have a didgeridoo what it was, either. I have absolutely no practical reason to be here except intrigue. And that it is something else to write about here. So let me tell you that the P&S is another of those little parts of the process that you'd never think of, just like redubbing the swearing with clean alternatives for planes. The P&S is for the benefit of dust-heads who will be watching the film on TV. So in order for the picture to fit the different shaped screens, you have to recompose the framing of all your shots (pan) and then rescan the resulting picture to give you a TV-friendly version of the film. With the rise of widescreen TVs, this practice is not as drastic as it was for the old square ones, but apparently you still have to do it for both ratios. Some regions in the world and some old aircraft still have the squarer 4:3 screens.

The session is at the same place where we did the grade. But we're not in a swish cinema suite with bionic chairs this time. We're in a little cupboard of a room in the bowels of the building with a normal TV screen. And befitting the Upstairs Downstairs nature of this session compared to the grade, the operator's London accent makes the director and I sound like Jeeves and effin Wooster. (And me and the director are pretty effin common, to be honest.)

He's good though, is the operator. He plays the film at double speed, as we're looking purely at composition. First we do the 16:9 version (for widescreen telly). This goes fairly smoothly, as most of the reframing is not hugely perceptible. And when there's a dialogue scene with two people in shot, we can either decide to favour one actor over another, or we can pan the picture a bit between the actors as each one speaks. Effectively adding a camera move. It's a fair solution, but apparently you don't want to do it too much as it will end up feeling like you got your cameraman from a Wimbledon tennis match. And there is one scene with three people in that proves quite difficult, but we do the best we can.

It's fine, but the overall result isn't nearly as cinematic as the cinema version. (So I highly recommend that you pay to watch it at the cinema if/when it comes out!)

Next, we look at the 4:3 version. The operator tells us that it is at this point that many film directors 'spit the dummy' and storm out of the room in disgust.

"Don't worry" says my director mate "I'm from advertising, I'm used to compromise".

Even so, this one feels a lot like a trip to the dentist. It has to be done, so one might as well assume the position and get it out of the way as quickly and painlessly as possible. It is tough making sure the titles fit in. The shots that were trying at 16:9 we have to be brutal with at 4:3. In fact, if we're not careful we could easily frame something out that will make the viewer lose comprehension of the story.

For example, in one dialogue scene, we decide we have to not favour either of the actors, and instead frame up on an inanimate object, because of its importance to the plot.

But much as I'd love to sit in a shitty little room watching my work being visually compromised all day, I've got a plane to catch. So I bid them farewell and pedal homeward. It's been raining and I'm knackered. So I take it easy. Besides, it's the middle of the day. There's much less traffic on the roads once I'm south of the river. I've got the bus lane all to myself on a long straight flat stretch between Surrey Quays and Deptford. I'll be home in ten mins at this steady pace, especially if that big red van doesn't pull out on m- BANG!

A Royal Mail van pulls out of a side road and hits me, side on. In the two seconds that it takes to happen, I notice the van, I notice him look right. I notice he doesn't notice me. He's looking up the road behind me. Then he pulls out.

I try my best to get past him as he does so, but the van whacks into the side of my bike, sending me clattering to the floor. I'm lucky. He didn't crash into my leg, but my back wheel. I still hit the ground hard. I'm lying in the middle of the road trying to work out if I'm all right and looking at my once immaculate bike, now scuffed and mangled. I'm absolutely livid.

"DID YOU NOT SEE ME? I'M WEARING A BRIGHT YELLOW HI-VIS JACKET, YOU DOZY TWAT!" I scream at the driver as he sheepishly gets out of the van.

I have to hand it to the guy. Despite being a terrible driver, he's good at being calm under pressure. His contrite demeanor does diffuse the situation enough for me to not want to throttle him. But I suppose it is easier to be calm when it's the company insurance, not his that is going to take a hit for this.

A fellow cyclist stops and asks me if I'm okay. I'm buzzing my tits off with adrenaline, so I don't know really. My arms and legs hurt and my hand and arm is grazed and bloody, but I'm able to stand, okay. So yeah, I'm okay. He helps me pick my bike off the road. He says he didn't see the incident though, so I let him go on his way. However, his Good Samaritan behavior is quickly erased when two women who are hanging over a balcony in the flats above shout down to me that he's just nicked my bike light and peddled off with it.

Wow, that's what you call an opportunist thief! What a wrong-un. I've a good mind to chase after him. Unfortunately my bike is not ride-able. The wheels are like bananas and I don't know how compromised the frame/forks/bars/gears are.

'Do you need an ambulance?' says the postman. I don't know if I do. But what I do know is, if an ambulance is called and they take me to A&E, I'll never make it to Gatwick in time. So I decline. He gives me his details. And I take photos of his van and the road name signs for good measure.

"It's okay, there's no damage to the van," he says, trying to keep things positive.

"Phew! I'm so chuffed you smashing into me didn't put a dent in your vehicle."

The blind twat isn't allowed passengers in his van, so I have to wander around with my broken two-wheeled pride and joy slung over my shoulders looking for a cab office. I could really do without this right now.

I don't have time to lick my wounds, or do any of the stuff I was going to do at home before the cab to the airport is due. I have to excuse myself from the work conference call, too. And to cap it all, the cab is late. To miss our flight after all that would be gutting.

However, the first bit of luck of the day comes my way - apart from being not dead - when there's a massive Police incident at the Dartford crossing, thereby leaving the rest of the motorway practically empty. Phew. As I finally relax in the back of the cab with the missus, I content myself that, where there's blame - and there is blame - there's a claim.

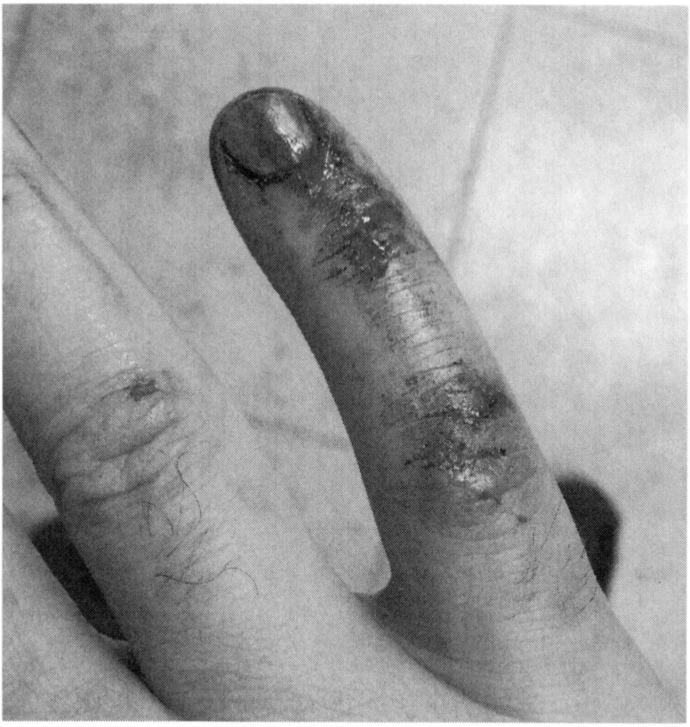

It's my suitcase carrying hand as well.

TRAILER TRASH

THE FIRST WEEK AT WORK after a holiday is always excruciating. I stroll in with my sunny disposition and relaxed attitude and walk straight into a whole world of workload and stress. BOSH! It's like a punch in the face. I immediately forget about all that lazing by the pool like Ray Whinstone in the opening sequence of Sexy Beast. I've got a shitload of important client comments to address. And the quicker I stop letting the perspective I've gained in my week off make me see it as pedantic and pointless servicing, the better.

And the weather has turned shite since I've been away. 'Poor me' I think as I negotiate Soho's Berwick Street Market in the relentless drizzle.

You could walk past the door I buzz a hundred times and not know it was there. I have. Today I'm not walking, I'm running late (with a post-cycling-crash gait). And when I take the lift to floor two, I realize that the inconspicuous door leads to a post-production facility that's half the size of Berwick Street. I've never even heard of the place, let alone worked here before, but it's blinking massive. So big, that the runner actually gets a bit lost as she shows me to the suite that my meeting is in.

I apologize for my lateness to the director, producers and the editor whose edit suite it is. He's going to be cutting our trailer for us. (He's not one of our film editors, he's a specialist trailer dude.) And we're here to discuss how the hell we're going to approach cutting a cool trailer for the film without giving away all the plot twists. Basically, the editor is saying that if we avoid using any of the dramatic plot twists, we're left with a pretty bland lot of clips that won't cut together into anything particularly exciting or motivating for the viewer. Thus defeating the object.

It's a toughie, because the equally valid counter argument is that if we give the plot twists away in the trailer, the film itself will not be nearly as enjoyable to watch. Given away plot twists are not known as 'spoilers' for nothing.

I just dunno. I've spent eighteen years having an opinion on the best way to promote products, but now when it's my own product, I have such a strong emotional attachment to it, I'm struggling to be in any way objective. And it's the same with the director, and the producers to an extent. We are all so bloody close to it.

But the editor isn't. He thinks that the best thing to do is to write some fresh material involving our main character and put together a trailer for the film comprised of existing film footage and newly shot stuff, together with a monologue that sets the right tone of intrigue and drama.

This is an unusual approach. And could be a good one. The director and I agree to consider the idea in principle, rather than wholeheartedly. As we need time to digest it before we can start writing anything. And we also go away and start looking at trailers of films with exciting plot twists to see if there are any approaches we could steal, sorry, be inspired by.

But I find it hard to even to think of any similar films. There are ones like Sixth Sense with one massive rug pull. But it's different to ours as it comes right at the end of the film. And it's got Bruce Willis in it. Our first carpet yank is after about twenty-five minutes. And it doesn't have Bruce Willis in it. And then there's The Crying Game, of course. But that carpet (snake) pull is right at the end, too.

The closest we find (it's of a similar genre, but still not as plot driven as ours) is Misery. Watch the trailer. It's interesting. You'll be surprised how much of the plot is in there. Even the sledgehammer on the ankles bit! So we're perhaps thinking that it might not be the end of the world to give a bit away in the trailer, after all.

But I'd still like to see how other comparable films have handled it in the past. I am having a 'just back from holiday, not quite with it' mental block.

CHOCOLATE BAR SHOOT

IT IS ALMOST A YEAR since we first started pitching for the chocolate bar account, and I am finally shooting an commercial for them.

After three rounds of research, we have managed to agree a script that the client, consumers, the research company and us at the agency all think is great.

Despite the over-scrutiny, we have arrived at a route that uses daftness to make our point to consumers. Great. And it means I've been able to attract a big name commercials director onto the project. I'm chuffed, because I've wanted to work with him for quite a few years, but this is the first time he's been up for directing a script that I've sent him.

One of the great things about advertising is you get to work with really interesting people and visit interesting places. And so I find myself on location in the middle of a deer reserve in Fife, Scotland, chatting to the director and his director of photography between takes.

The director is a good-natured Swedish man. The director of photography is an unassuming elderly Polish man. A pipe smoker, who also happens to have been Quentin Tarantino's director of photography on films such as Reservoir Dogs and Pulp Fiction.

The brilliant surreal-ness of the situation is as tangible to my senses as the pipe smoke filling my nostrils and the Scotch mist rolling across my eye line.

I have decided not to dent their enthusiasm by passing on the news I received four days ago. The media budget for the commercial (the money to broadcast the ad on TV) has been pulled for the year, so it will not run for another six months.

Luckily for us, the media budget decision was made after the production budget had been signed off. Otherwise, I suspect we wouldn't be standing here now filming an imperious herd of deer striding across the countryside.

It's a lovely feeling being on set again, especially in such a life-affirming area of outstandingly bad phone reception, which means I am not contactable by anyone at the office.

Even after a lot of years of coming up with ideas for a living, it's still a huge buzz stepping onto a set and seeing all the equipment and the crew buzzing around, just because little old me wrote something silly down on a piece of paper.

Despite the 'death by paper cuts' nature of some of these projects, when you're on set, it all becomes worth it. Like with the movie, perseverance has been rewarded.

It's a shame our on-set caterers don't share this karmic state of mind, however. My colleagues and I had resolved not to eat any venison on this trip out of respect for the majestic beasts we are filming, but the caterers go and serve us venison stew for lunch. Shit. Bad vibes, man. But it tastes bloody lovely and, to be fair, it doesn't seem to put any karmic catastrophe onto the shoot, or the trip in general.

During the two shooting days, we pretty much have to remain silent so as not to freak out the deer. This contrives to make the evenings that bit more raucous.

We're talking lock-ins in pubs, drunkenly stealing mannequins from hotel souvenir shops, drinking whisky from the bottle in a field at four a.m. That kind of stuff. And fair play, the client is with us pretty much every drunken step of the way.

But by the time we get on the train at Edinburgh on Saturday morning, I've had a month's worth of drinking and a night's worth of sleep in a week, and I need to get back home and 'chill the fuck oot' (as Davey, our driver for the week, would say).

CAST AND CREW SCREENING

THE VERY MOMENT the alarm goes off I regret letting my mates drink me out of house and home until four a.m. last night (and eating my all my cheese reserves). Living on a street with four pubs on it means quite a few Saturday nights turn into a party at ours after closing time. This is exactly how we like it, of course. And we normally like the accompanying midday lie-ins, too. But not this Sunday. It's eight-thirty effin a.m. Me and the missus are up. We've showered, roused our mate who dossed on the sofa, fed the cat, and greeted our daughter as she arrives home from her all-night shift at a nightclub*. We have ordered a taxi and got dressed. (Not in that order.)

We have to be at the Curzon Cinema on Shaftsbury Avenue in the west end of London for a ten effin a.m. screening of the film. It's the Cast and Crew Screening. The first time the finished article has ever been shown to an audience. And as the title suggests, it's the part of the process where all the people who worked on the film get to see it.

If I'm nervous, the splitting headache and faintly nauseous feeling from my hangover masks it successfully. Again, it's not the tuxedo and red carpet affair you'd perhaps expect it to be. The crack of sparrows on a Sunday isn't the most glamorous of screening times. But it's purely a financial thing. West End cinemas charge, what, fifteen quid a throw? Multiply that by three hundred seats and you're talking, err, a lot of money... four and a half grand, or so, per showing? Add the popcorn/hot dog/drinks/Poppets sales and it's no wonder commercial cinemas are not cheap to hire. So it's understandable that most C&C screenings are held at times of the day not conducive to eveningwear. But it's really great to see everyone again. And I'm not the only one with a hangover, judging by the amount of people clutching bottles of water in the foyer.

Despite this dream of a project being a reality for seven months now, I still can't help letting the excited film fan inside me come out. As well as the water, I clutch my copy of the shooting script that I've held onto since the shoot. And I get everyone to sign it for me. Everyone obliges, some of them accompanied by very nice personal messages. In fact it's only the director and producer who write anything rude. (Or draw something rude, in the producer's case. If that's what your private parts looks like, mate, I suggest you see a doctor.)

But the clock's ticking, so we are quickly ushered into screen one. I sit down with my missus and our guests (a close friend and my missus' fav aunty), but the producers and the director beckon me to join them up on stage. This is at once a touching and excruciating moment. Touching to be included, excruciating to be in the spotlight.

One of the producers does the introductions, before handing over to the director to say a few words. And given that he finds it even more excruciating than me, he does exactly that – says only a few words.

Unaccustomed as I am to being awake at ten a.m. on a Sunday morning, I refrain from giving a speech. But I do blurt out that we'll be in De Hems afterwards. (The Dutch pub, which is a few paces away from the theatre in Chinatown. You know the one.) But I suppose it would have been nice if I'd articulated how brilliant it has been to work with so many talented, professional, funny people.

Obviously, we'll never get an easier audience than a room full of people who worked on the bloody thing. So saying that it played really well is not exactly a barometer of the quality of the film. But the vibe in the room is good. Afterwards, people are really enthusiastic in their praise, which is lovely. And a lot of them do say they would tell me if they thought it was shit. Which is good enough for me. Intoxicated by all the positivity flying about and the joy of seeing so many great people again, I make light work of the hair of the dog that bit me. And before I know it, I've had a whole furry skin full in the wooden shoe-wearers' boozer and we're going for a Chinese. (I *must* be drunk if I'm going for a Chinese.)

It's been a special day. It really has. I even get to have a lie-in on the sofa when I get home. And when I wake up, I wear my second awful hangover of the day with absolute pride.

* *My stepdaughter worked on the film in the wardrobe department, and appeared in the film as an extra, so she would have been at the C&C if it wasn't for the night shift.*

CHAMPAGNE RECEPTION

DESIRABLE AS A THREE-THIRTY Monday finish undoubtedly is, it's not something you get to do in an office job very often. So it is with great pleasure - and great theatre for the benefit of one's colleagues - that I saunter over to the coat-stand and slip on my jacket with a satisfaction usually reserved for Masters golf champions.

This public disregard for office hours may seem foolhardy, but never fear, I am on solid ground. For my early disappearance is to be accompanied by my superiors. Brilliant, and fair dos. Having sanctioned my six-week 'sabbatical' for the shoot, and my 'flexible' approach to my timetable all summer to incorporate the post-production, the least I could do is invite my bosses to a screening at the earliest opportunity.

Today is that opportunity. It's the first showing of the finished film to anyone not directly involved in its production. It's an industry screening to potential distribution partners. It's the first step on the road to getting the bloody thing on at the cinema. As I step out of the agency with my two betters and take the fifteen-minute stroll to the screening room venue with them, I admit to being a little nervous. One of the great things about the film project has been the lack of an agency creative approvals process*.

But all the same, I REALLY want the guys to approve of my extra-curricular efforts today.

Then there's the small matter of the important industry people who are also invited. And the BLA (brilliant leading actress). She was filming on the day of the Cast and Crew screening, so hasn't seen the finished film yet. So I'm a bit anxious.

The producers have hired a small thirty-five-seat screening room on Charlotte Street (which is near Soho, but north of Oxford Street). It's full of bars and restaurants, and is also home to one of the most famous ad agencies (basically, it's the only one that people not in advertising have heard of). It's the ad agency where, eighteen years ago, I had my first ever work placement as a student advertising creative.

Jesus. It's been a long journey to get where I am today – basically a couple of doors away. And I'm still a bloody rookie! (Albeit in a different game.) Mind you, if the forty-year-old me ever got to go back and tell the 1995 ad student me that in the future I'd be standing in a posh foyer enjoying a champagne reception with a famous actress and a dozen leading film industry figures ahead of a screening of a feature film I'd written, I would surely have found it even more ridiculous than shit like smartphones, Skype calls, Man City being good, Jim'll Fix-It a paedophile etc. (Jim never fixed it for me. But then again, my teachers did always say I had very grown-up handwriting.)

The young me would also have urged me to exercise more and stay off the pies. And he would have tapped me up for a few quid, too, the cheeky young scamp. So I'm glad the athletic, dark haired little oik is not here, because I need to mingle. But mingling isn't my forte.

As I try my pathetic best to 'work' the room, I can see my bosses out of the corner of my eye stood at the bar. I can tell they are ripping the piss out of my woeful shmoozery. The fuckers. But what can I do? At least I don't need to get up at the front of the theatre this time, when everyone takes their seats. The producer does the honours. He apologises for the director's absence, as he is on holiday.

'What, again?!' shouts out the BLA, which makes me, and quite a few others, laugh. Then the lights go down. And here we go. I sit at the back. I still enjoy watching it, but I find myself looking for the faults more with every viewing. But seeing as there are people we want to impress here, I still do my best to gasp, audibly wince and laugh at all the appropriate moments to help the ambience of the room. The industry people sitting to my immediate right and left do, too. So that's good. Or is it? It's bloody hard to tell, to be honest.

As we stream back into the brightly lit foyer afterwards, there are a lot of happy faces and polite handshakes going on. But Christ knows how it will stand us in stead, business-wise. It is always so, according to our producers, who are veterans of this sort of thing. So we'll see.

As far as non-industry members of the audience are concerned, the reactions are a lot more emphatic. My bosses are either very convincing actors or they genuinely like it. Chuffed! One of them comments that he could 'see a lot of me in there'. I hope he meant that as a good thing.

The BLA's agent and actress friend are full of praise, too. The BLA is happy and a bit overwhelmed, I think. But I suppose you would be after watching yourself on a massive screen for an hour and a half (she is in every single scene of the film, bar one, remember). At the pub, afterwards, I ask her if she finds it difficult to watch herself on screen and she admits that it's hard not to be self-critical. She's got nothing to be self-critical about from where I'm sitting.

Where I'm sitting also happens to be in the same pub that I used to frequent whilst on student placement all those years ago. Back then I'd always do my best to find a Creative Director to ponce a pint off. Some things never change.

**As a creative person in advertising, everything we do has to be approved internally by the Creative Director(s) before it is shown to the client. Everything. From a script for a million pound commercial, to the choice of voiceover artist for a little radio ad. Basically, every creative decision, big or small, has to be approved by a CD. The Creative Director (or Executive Creative Director, or Chief Creative Officer, or whatever the current job title, de jour, right now) is the creative quality controller of the whole agency output. There are also 'group head' Creative Directors who look after certain client accounts (I do this kind of CD-ing, myself). But these CDs still need to seek approval from THE Creative Director(s) of the agency.*

It's a good process when handled correctly. The constant scrutiny keeps everyone honest and standards high. But it can be fucking tedious at times. Especially when you're a grey-haired old see-you-en-tee, like myself. So it's been a nice antidote to not have to seek approval for everything the whole time whilst writing and working on the film.

This is, obviously, nothing personally to do with my bosses. They are great blokes, as it goes. Nor is it anything against any other of the Creative Directors I've worked into over the years. Well, there have been one or two talentless, egotistical bullies along the way. But in the main, most of them are pretty sound.

AWARDS SCHM-AWARDS

SO WE'VE DECIDED on the approach for the trailer. After watching lots of other movie trailers of a similar genre, we've realised that most films don't mind giving stuff in the plot away. As long as there is a bit of abstraction to it and it paints its own exciting/intriguing picture, rather than just showing a cut-down of the whole film in a hundred and twenty seconds. Basically, not giving TOO, too much away. So, with that in mind, I've written a monologue for our BLA (brilliant lead actress) to deliver in voiceover to the pictures. This is unusual. Most trailers either use titles, or some sort of cheesy American movie voiceover. You know the type...

'IN A WORLD OF FEISTY CAREER WOMEN... SHE WAS ON A COLLISION COURSE WITH DESTINY... bla bla etcetera etcetera.

Seeing as the film doesn't feature Steven Segal in any of the roles, I'm going with the monologue option. The director, producers are in agreement, so we've left it with the editor for half a week so he can weave his magic.

In the mean time, I have the (dubious) pleasure of dressing up for a black tie advertising awards ceremony tonight. I say dress up.

Dark jeans, scuffed shoes, a shirt and blazer is as close to 'black tie' as I can possibly manage.

It's fine, though. Being a 'creative' gives you plenty of latitude with dress codes. It's a big part of why I chose it as a career path, as it goes.

For those of you who have never been to an advertising award ceremony, let me explain. They are exactly the same as those glamorous and glitzy award ceremonies you see on TV, like The BAFTA's, The Turner Prize of The Mercury. And like their famous counterparts, they are held in amazing locations, filled with beautiful people eating expensive food, quaffing fine wine (and no doubt hoovering illicit powders). They are also hosted by a famous wit like a Stephen Fry or a Jimmy Carr. And the trophies are things of beauty. Yes, the only real difference is that we're awarding adverts not films, art or music.

There's even a Cannes festival for advertising. Held every year, after the Cannes Film Festival and also after the Cannes International Porn Festival. I am sure they are not held in their hierarchy of importance. Definitely not. No.

The awards night I'm attending is at The Grosvenor House Hotel on Park Lane, which is the best place to have a hotel in London, as anyone who's ever played Monopoly will know.

The function room at the Grosvenor House, known as The Great Room, is like an awards function factory. For every glitzy extravaganza that is beamed to our telly boxes, there are probably a hundred equally glitzy, yet nowhere near as glamorous awards ceremonies taking place there, every night of the week. In every single industry you can imagine, and loads more industries you probably couldn't.

Okay, advertising is a commercial art, not art. But at least there's a kind of artistic merit involved in it that can be judged and awarded subjectively. It's not like the Chicken Cottage Awards, or the Practitioners in Double Glazing Awards, is it? Or is it?

Thankfully, the one thing we don't do at advertising awards dos, is the acceptance speech. I thank Our Lord Jesus Christ that no-one has to hear some agency person thanking Our Lord Jesus Christ for winning best consumer durables direct response radio ad, or some-such. But we do take them very seriously.

Whole advertising careers are defined by success (or lack of) at advertising award shows. Particularly for creative people. As young creatives entering the business we buy in to the idea that promotions, pay rises and respect from our peers come from winning awards. We are conditioned to chase them obsessively.

As a not-so-young ad man, I don't tend to go to award dos now unless I am actually shortlisted to win an award. Tonight I am. In the Grocery, Soft Drinks & Household, Interactive category, I'll have you know. It's for a Twitter-based campaign I did for a well-known condiment brand. Oh, the glamour. I'm not expecting to win, as there is stiff competition in the category from a digital campaign for a well-known household cleaning brand (that used to share its name with a squeezy lemon brand until recently changing its name by one letter).

Again, oh the glamour.

As soon as I arrive at The Great Room with my colleagues, I realizc I'm not going to win tonight. Our table is nowhere effin near the effin stage. So there's only one thing for it – we wade right into the effin booze.

Another thing about The Great Room is it is effectively in the basement of the hotel. Getting a signal on your phone is near impossible. So only one of our table is able to take advantage of the live Twitter facility that sends all correctly hash-tagged tweets to the big screens above the stage.

Despite the inevitable happening and the cleaning product campaign cleaning up in my category, it's a good night. (Fair enough, it was better than my effort. Must try harder). It's nice to see a few old faces. There's a lot of good work awarded, as well as a few not so good 'uns. At this point, it's customary for people who don't win at advertising awards dos to say that the standard of work that won is not as good as last year/five years/ten years ago (usually corresponding with the last time they won one). But that's just sour grapes. I don't do sour grapes.

It would also be sour grapes to point out that the chairman of the judges is the co-founder of the agency that picked up the most awards tonight. So I won't.

And I won't be calling it a fucking racket, either. I don't do sour grapes. Besides, I used to work at that agency. I know and like some of the people that won tonight. So I wouldn't want to take the shine off their victories. IDDSG. (Because MBAA)*

But I do think that the best bit of writing that appeared on the big screen tonight wasn't any of the winning ads. It was my workmate's tweet of:

'Is anyone moderating these fucking cunting tweets?'

** Movie beats advertising award.*

TRAILER

I HAVEN'T UPDATED this for a while. Sorr-eeeeee. This is partly because I am busy with the old nine-to-five. (Jesus, It would be lovely if the hours were just nine-to-five.) And partly because nothing much has happened on the film front to report. Well, I say nothing. Plenty is happening, but it's business stuff. And I don't want to ruin anything by shooting my big mouth off about it prematurely. But sorry for being cryptic.

Talking of which, we've ummed and ahhed about how cryptic the trailer should or shouldn't be for quite a while. But we've got one cut now. To be honest, it does actually give a fair bit of the plot away. But fair play to our trailer editor dude, it is exciting. And I think much of the stuff that's revealed in there is either abstract enough to not actually give anything away, or presented in a way that gives it a different context to how it appears in the actual film.

The most impressive and unexpected thing that the editor has done, is that he's managed to not include the main surprise in the film – a plot twist after roughly twenty-four minutes, thirty-five seconds* that changes the whole course of the story. To do that and still make the trailer pretty exciting is a feat.

People I've showed it to, so far, seem to respond well. Mostly, these are mates who've seen the film (or at least a rough version of it, anyway). But a few I've shown it to don't know a thing about the story and like it.

The only niggle I have is that by omitting such a big part of the story, we're slightly misrepresenting the film. You could argue it's selling a different film, if you were being harsh. It's all done for the good of the viewing experience of the film itself, of course. Besides, the purpose of the trailer is purely to get people to buy a ticket. The trailer's good, as is. But a part of me wonders if it would be even more exciting and motivating if the bit in question were to be included. Pros and cons. Pros and cons.

If I'm sounding like a shit indecisive advertising client right now, it's because I'm behaving like one. But in the spirit of a shit indecisive advertising client who shows rough edits of commercials around their whole goddam company before they can make a decision**, I'd love to show it to you now to see what you think. But it needs a sound mix, a bit of post work and a monologue to go over some of the picture, delivered by our leading lady (rather then the editor's dulcet guide voiceover that's on there at the moment).

Perhaps I should get the editor dude to go again, but include the other bit in the plot this time. Then I can compare the two side-by-side. Perhaps I could show both versions to lots of people and ask them questions about it. A research group, even. Basically, I could get a consensus of unqualified opinion to tell me what to do, rather than using my own judgment and expertise to make any decision, ever. Oh yeah, I'm behaving like a shit indecisive advertising client, all right.

* *Don't you just love people who say things like 'it's about thirteen minutes past...'? Does that make them a pedant for being so precise, or me a pedant for being irritated by it?*

** *Any similarity with any client I have formerly or am currently working with, living or dead, is purely coincidental. And this is by no means a sly dig at anyone who directly or indirectly pays my wages and, therefore, my mortgage.*

MORE FILMING

Apparently, fifteen feature films are launched every week in the UK*. So, whenever we launch our film, we'll be competing with a lot of others to be the movie that cinemagoers choose as their night out that week.

Of course, we'll be at a huge disadvantage to most of our rivals. Many of them will be big studio pictures starring huge Hollywood stars with massive fan-bases, and/or directed by famous critically acclaimed auteurs. Some of them may be written by big-name screenwriters, or have a load of film awards and five-star ratings on their posters. They will be big budget films, with big marketing budgets to promote them.

It doesn't make them better films than ours (or worse). But as you know, ours is made by a couple of no-marks from advertising. And although it stars two household names, they are well known from the world of television, not film. We won't have a huge marketing budget, and we can't rely on winning any awards. So all we've got is the hope of some kind film reviews to help us get on people's consideration list.

Because, when selecting a movie to watch, we look to the pedigree of the actors and filmmakers, and the critical acclaim it has received.

It's true. Think about what drives your decision to watch one flick over another next time you go to the pictures. Me and the missus did it ourselves last night. We were at a loose end, so we wandered down to the end of the road to our local Picturehouse cinema. (I consider having a decent cinema at the end of my street one of my greatest luxuries.) In absence of reading any reviews this week, we ended up watching Nebraska**. Our reasons were:

1. We liked the poster.
2. It was directed by the same bloke who made Sideways.
3. The star won Best Actor at Cannes and the film was nominated for the Palme D'or.

It all goes to show we need to think really hard about other ways to get our film noticed. We're not going to get on many people's consideration list using the usual methods. We need to get ourselves a fan-base ahead of release. Create a buzz, somehow, so people want to seek it out. That's what we're thinking, anyway. So I've had an idea that will, hopefully, make some noise and get us some interest.

Without going into any detail whatsoever, it involves filming extra scenes that are in the story but not in the film. It's called the 'Meanwhile Project'. Basically, we're filming our characters in new scenes that happen in parallel to ones in the film. (As in 'Meanwhile, on the other side of London...')

I don't know if that makes any sense, but anyway, we're filming one of them today. It's with our excellent lead male actor. We're lucky to get him, because he's about to jump on a plane to Australia. No, not as a contestant of 'I'm a Celebrity, Get Me Out of Here', but to shoot his next feature film***. So quite a lot more glamorous than Streatham in the pissing rain. We have no circus of lighting trucks, camera trucks, runners, producers, make-up, wardrobe, sparks, art department, catering etc.

It's just the director, a producer, a cameraman and the actor. He looks knackered. Having a six-week-old at home kind of does that to you. But he's on good form. And the scene is really easy for him. He gives us the seriously nasty bastard performance we're looking for, and we knock it off in half an hour. Blimey, we've just shot a one-minute ad in thirty minutes. Amazing. Quickest ad shoot I've ever been on. Must be because I'm the client. Oh, and because the actor's effin brilliant.

I thought I'd be out for more than half a day, but I'm back in the office before eleven a.m. Brilliant, because I am really busy putting the finishing touches to the chocolate bar commercial I've been working on for well over a year.

* *I know, it seems like a hell of a lot. I'm just repeating what I've been told.*

** *Nebraska is good. It is a 'loser road movie' like Sideways. It's not as good, as Sideways, though. It's quite slow, but slow on purpose. It actually feels kind of boring at first, but once you get into its peculiar rhythm, it is enjoyable.*

It's about family, aging, disappointment and pride. It's tender and quietly funny. And it has 'Saul' from Breaking Bad in one of the supporting roles, which is a bit of a bonus.

Oh, and it's shot in B&W, which probably makes it feel a bit more artful and timeless than it actually is. But who do I think I am, Barry Norman? I enjoyed it.

**** The film is the second spin-off movie from the comedy TV series that made him famous. Big budget.*

MORE MORE FILMING

IT'S A TOUGH WEEK AT WORK. I'm working on a new business pitch at the moment. For anyone reading this who isn't in advertising, a new business pitch is the process whereby a client invites several ad agencies to pitch for their advertising account. To ad agency folk, it's an opportunity to run around like headless chickens working stupidly long hours, drinking too much coffee, eating shit takeaway food, pulling all-nighters and generally putting their lives on hold in order to produce three years worth of advertising in two weeks. Sounds like a nightmare, and it is. It can also be a lot of fun. Well, the lunch after the presentation is. And the drink-up if you win. And the drink-up if you lose.

Ordinarily, the prospect of getting up early on a Saturday, the only day I know I'm going to be having off in the midst of this pitch, would piss me right off. Instead, I'm quite cheery as I stroll to the station. (Quite cheery for me, anyway.)

Today we're doing some more filming for our 'meanwhile project'. It's with our BLA (brilliant leading actress) today. And we're back at one of the locations we shot at when we were in production. It's in the City of London. Feels odd to be back. For a start it's not snowing, and being a Saturday morning in The City, it's deserted. Crew-wise, there are only seven of us here today. There were one hundred and twenty-seven of us last time, including half my family as extras. Still, it's nice to see the seven who are here – cameraman, actress, two producers, make-up lady, director, and writer.

I crack the joke that it's a shame I didn't think of this project earlier, as we could have knocked it off during production and saved a few quid. The producers agree with me (a bit too whole-heartedly). What can I say? I'm on a learning curve here. But I swear to them that the next time they give me a once-in-a-lifetime opportunity I will have a good think about the promotional activity ahead of production.

Like last time with our leading man, it's a simple scene we're shooting today. And like last time, our actor throws herself into it and nails it in no time. Boom. Easy as that. Great news, but it means that when she suggests we go for a pint to celebrate, the pubs aren't actually open yet.

Luckily, our producer is a Soho House member (which, for those not in advertising or any other wanky media profession, is a members-only club for wanky media professionals). So once the actress is back in her civvies, we decide to take a ten-minute stroll to the Soho House branch in Shoreditch, which is appropriately named Shoreditch House. It's housed in an old building formerly used as a tea warehouse. They share the building with an ad agency. Someone told me that the building is actually owned by the bloke who owns the ad agency. And that he makes more money in rent than he does from the agency. It might be true, but then again, the bloke who told me is in advertising, and therefore cannot be trusted.

Anyway, we stroll in and sign in. We get in the lift with a couple that are wearing terry-toweling robes. No it's not that kind of club. There is a swimming pool on the roof. I've been here several times before, but usually drunk and at night. I must say it's a very pleasant atmosphere and the eggs benedict goes down beautifully with the Guinni (plural of Guinness). I'm having a nice time. I even bump into one of my colleagues from work. He is a young hipster East London type, and he wears an odd smile as we chat, that I swear says 'what is an old fucker like you doing in a place like this, hanging out with a famous person?'

Or he might just have been smiling. I'm probably reading too much into it, to be honest.

Anyway, when I finally need to 'break the seal' after three pints – the director and actress call me a camel – I really notice the difference between the nighttime and daytime atmospheres here. For one, I don't have to wade through loads of people waiting to snort powders in the toilets. And while wandering past another part of the club, I come across the ridiculously pleased-with-itself sight of thirty or so couples and their young kids having some sort of posh parents and toddlers club meeting.

Jesus, the value of the pushchairs alone probably rivals that of the average car dealership forecourt. I suppose this scene is much like every single Café Rouge across the country at this time on a Saturday. Albeit an elitist version. Funny, I would have thought that the whole point of a members club is a retreat from places swarming with screaming kids. But what do I know? I haven't got young kids. I'm not cool. And I've drunk too much Guinness. I'd better shut up and order another pint.

ANOTHER INDUSTRY SCREENING

WE HAVE ANOTHER industry screening today (hence the title). Even though I am now on holiday from work until after Christmas - get in - I turn up late. Bad me. So I miss the pre-screening Champagne and small talk. These industry screenings are a bit odd, to be honest.

Held in tiny screening rooms that seat thirty people, or so, they are not like screenings we've had with normal audiences. These ones are filled with film industry people who are not here to be entertained. They're here purely to gauge whether they think they can make money out of it, or not. Consequently, many of the bits in the film where the test audiences were gasping, laughing, or shrieking provoke little or no audible reaction here. It freaked me out the first time we did an industry screening. I now understand, but it still bothers me. So I make sure I invite some friends along, to make the atmosphere in the room a little more authentic.

It being a weekday afternoon, several of my invitees end up dropping out. (If you're reading this, you're dead to me.) In the end only two show up. They're female. I'm happy with this, as I reckon they are likely to be a bit 'shrieky'.

Thankfully, my sweeping generalisation is proved right, and

the atmosphere in the room is much improved by their presence. Not that you know if these things actually go well or not until days/weeks after, when people either indicate interest or pass.

As I stand in the foyer with the producers afterwards, trying to read the poker faces of the departing industry types, I spot a few other familiar faces.

One's a commercials director I know. There are a couple of other bods from the ad production company that the director runs. And there's another guy - an ad copywriter - who I haven't seen for quite a while.

The writer bloke played a very important role in this project, as it goes. For, it was he who first introduced us to our producer.

He reminds me that the last time we met was exactly one year ago, on the occasion of the Table Read*.

Time flies. This time last year I booked a day off work and turned up at the producer's house along with my director mate and a dozen others. Half a dozen of them were actors, there to perform a read-through of the script. The rest of us - me, the director, the producers and a couple of respected independent witnesses - were here to listen, take notes and discuss if any improvements could be made.

Nightmare.

The producer's homemade lasagne was first rate. The wine was well selected. The read-through itself went well. It was a good exercise to hear it all read out and the lines performed by actors. I took a couple of notes along the way about things I should tweak, but not much. And actually, most of the actors and witnesses, including the copywriter guy, only had positive feedback. But just like in an advertising research focus group, one opinionated so-and-so can spoil the atmosphere and objectivity of the whole thing.

Many times I've wanted to jump through the one-way glass of a research facility and throttle some jumped-up, axe grinding, soapbox standing moron who is single-handedly messing up the chances of one of my adverts getting made.

There is no one-way glass to wring my hands behind here. I have to smile and take it on the chin as one of the actors totally assassinates my plot and characters.

Jesus, I practically skipped along to this session in anticipation of a wonderful new experience. I come out feeling beaten up and thoroughly depressed. As I recall, at that point I wasn't sure whether we had the funding in place for production or not. Apart from the ego bashing, I was worried that the guy's tirade might make the producers lose faith and ask me to do a big re-write.

I needn't have worried. They didn't agree with him, either. We ploughed on, and here I am. Twelve months later, clinking Champagne glasses with my copywriter friend in the foyer of a private cinema. Happy days.

Actually, REALLY happy days, because after bidding farewell to my fellow copywriter and having a quick drink with my two guests - my sister-in-law and her friend - I then repair to the nearest football pub to meet my best pal and get nicely sozzled while watching the Mighty Hammers put Spurs to the sword in a cup game. As I stumble Tube-wards in the drizzle with the glow of victory and a post-match celebratory chicken jalfrezi warming me, I dare to dream that the highly critical bloke from the Table Read is a Spurs fan.

* *The table read is the first live read-through of the screenplay, performed by actors sitting around a table and with a narrator reading out the direction narrative). It's an opportunity for the producers, director and writer to hear the material come to life. It serves as a way of identifying problems with the script, like wooden dialogue, boring bits or unsmooth scene transitions. We hadn't started the casting process at this point, so none of the actors from the film were there. (We did a cast read-through nearer the shoot.)*

THIS TIME LAST YEAR

IT IS A CRISP, BRIGHT, DRY Sunday afternoon. I'm having a lovely weekend of doing large amounts of fuck-all*. Great. I've just spent the first two weeks back from Christmas working like a nutter on an advertising new business pitch, so I could do with a rest. I won't tell you the name of the brand I've been pitching for. For one, there's a degree of client confidentiality involved. And there's also the fact that it's not a particularly glamorous brand. I'd still like to win it, of course**.

Anyway, it's certainly nice to stroll through Greenwich Park with the missus without any stress hanging over me. As we walk, I am reminded of a similar Sunday stroll we took in this park a year ago. Same weather, same time of year. The only difference being that this time last year I had a knot in my stomach. It was a big 'un. The type only a scout leader could tie. Not in a dodgy 'let me help you with your woggle' scout leader way, just an impressive, highly sophisticated, hard-to-untie knot.

If I recall correctly, by this stage we'd secured the financing for the film's production. We'd found the prime location to shoot it - a 17th floor apartment on the Isle of Dogs - and we were now in the thick of the casting process.

That's why I was in turmoil.

The feature film casting process is a tortuous one. I had no idea*** it was such a ball ache, but I quickly realised that you can't just send your script out to loads of actors and hope that one of them is interested. Oh no. There is a massive unwritten ego-massaging procedure to follow. A protocol that means you must offer the part to potential lead actors/actresses one at a time, in order of their hierarchy in the industry.

As far as I can tell, the protocol is as follows...

You draw a list. You put the biggest star you would like at the top and you work your way down the list in order of their industry profile. This can be a list of two, or as long as your arm. But it's a list, a list in which you cannot offer the part to more than one person at a time. So, for example, you can't offer a part to Kate Winslet and Tilda Swinton at the same time. And say you send it to Kate and she passes, you probably couldn't then send it to Tilda, because as someone with a similar profile, it would be insulting to send her one of Kate's cast-offs.

Also, you can't start lower by sending it to, say, a Carey Mulligan and then send it to Kate Winslet, because that would be disrespectful of Kate's higher profile. No, you'd have to offer it to Kate OR Tilda. Then, if that's a pass, you'd maybe go to Helena Bonham-Carter, then to Carey Mulligan, and so on and so on down your list until you end up sending it to Kat Slater from Eastenders. Oh yeah, it's an intricate, minefield chess match of a process, all right.

And it's not just a case of pinging e-mails and getting responses in a day or so. Each one can take weeks.

So in December we had drawn up a list of British actresses to play our lead***. We had a casting agent who helped draw up the list and played the game on behalf of the producers, dealing with the theatrical agents who in turn work on behalf of the actors. At the top were Oscar winners, at the bottom were hugely talented actors, but with much lower profiles.

We had no real thought in our minds that the person at the top would be interested. (The part is a great one for a woman - she is in every single scene of the film, bar one - but it's a small low budget film written and directed by complete unknowns.) However, seeing as the worst thing she could do was say 'no', we gave it a shot.

She didn't say 'no'. She was unavailable. Funnily enough, top people don't tend to sit at home twiddling their thumbs waiting for scripts to come in.

So we went to number two on our list. This person is huge, but there was no way she was right for the part, in my opinion. So I was quite chuffed when her agent soon passed on her behalf.

Everyone liked number three on the list. She's an Oscar-nominee of high critical acclaim. She read the script. She liked it. She was interested. She was thinking about it. I was absolutely wetting myself with excitement.

She kept thinking about it. I ran out of wee wee to wet myself with. She thought about it some more. It emerges that the problem was, she also had another script on the table that she liked. It wasn't nearly as good a part as ours. (In my non-humble opinion. The other film was only a co-star part.) And it was a six-week shoot in Germany, which wasn't conducive to her being a mother of young kids. Ours was a fantastic part for a middle-aged woman. It was a mere four-week shoot and the location was a piffling ten-minute cab ride from her home. In fact, the only thing that the other film had going for it was that it paid ten times more money than ours would have done.

It got to week three of her thinking about it and me dry-wetting myself with excitement. Someone said that actresses sometimes hold onto scripts for months so that other actresses don't get offered the part and they get to hedge their bets until something bigger and better comes along. We had a specific shoot date planned. We couldn't eff around like this. Excitement turned to anxiety. I couldn't concentrate in my day job. I couldn't concentrate on anything. Even a relaxing walk around the park on a crisp Sunday afternoon couldn't loosen the Baden-Powell-esque knot in my stomach.

It was an exquisitely horrible feeling, as it goes. And it continued beyond the moment when she finally passed on the script, right up until the day we confirmed our actual lead actress several weeks later.

It's funny thinking back, after subsequently finding an actress who we're extremely honoured to have worked with. Admittedly, she is not as high profile on an international scale, but is a big deal in this country. And is easily as strong a performer as absolutely anyone on the list. I certainly can't imagine anyone else but the person we have starring in the film. We did really well to get her. And far be it from me to blow my own trumpet (I'd need to get a rib removed before I could manage that), but it was my idea to approach her in the first place. Oh yeah, they all come around to my way of thinking in the end*****.

** I did eff-all except watch West Ham get beat by Newcastle at Upton Park, but one doesn't wish to dwell on negatives.*

*** I've subsequently discovered that we lost the pitch. Damn! It was a protracted process that began five months ago with a 'chemistry meeting'. This is where the client meets lots of agencies and gets a feel for which ones they could see themselves working with/bossing about.*

Then, a few weeks later we were invited to the strategy and creative work stage against five other agencies. After this, the client then contacted us saying no agency had quite 'hit the spot', but they'd like ourselves and one other agency to do another round of work. We agreed, worked our tits off for another couple of weeks, but ended up coming second. So basically, we did a hell of a lot of hard work for nothing. I'll never get that time back. It was going to be a huge part of my pay rise argument, as well. If I had gone ahead and farted in the chemistry meeting all those months ago, I could have saved myself a lot of unnecessary pain.

**** The casting process in the advertising world is much more straightforward than films. You have a casting agent. They pull in a load of actors. You hire a casting suite for a day (basically an empty room with a video camera) and get loads of actors to come in and audition. You pick your favourite two or three with the director. You then sell your first choice to the client. (With the other one or two as back-ups.) Of course, we use famous people in ads, too. But you'd never get them in to read for a part. Quite often, they are signed up prior to the ad being written, anyway.*

**** *The authors of the list for the lead actress were the director, two producers and the casting agent. As the director's mate, I had a lot of input with casting suggestions, but wasn't physically in the meetings with the casting agent. Fair dos. Writers never usually get involved in this sort of thing. I didn't want to step on any toes, or nuffink.*

***** *Apart from the client of the advertising account I've just pitched for, of course.*

WAITING GAME

GOOD THINGS COME to those who wait. It's true. It must be. The famous advertising slogan says so. As someone who has been sucking Satan's cock* for twenty years now, I believe it wholeheartedly. I have to. Some of the commercial projects I work on take months and months to come to fruition. I've been working on the chocolate bar project for a year and a half, and the ad still hasn't gone on air, yet.

We got the commercial finished, but as you may remember, they cut the media budget. It's been a disaster, because in the time it has been sitting on the shelf, it has had plenty of time to be over analysed by loads of different people and chipped away at.

Also, the client who actually bought the script has taken another job. His replacement is not a fan of the work and has forced us to make several edit changes that make it nowhere near as good as it was. Then, the commercial was put in front of consumers for the fourth round of research. And guess what? The new edit that they made us cut has not performed well in research. And it's our fault.

This is a bit like if I took my car to the garage (if I had a car) and told them they need to fix the clutch. And despite them – the experts – saying the problem is actually the gearbox, insisting that they do as they are told and fix the clutch. And when subsequently my gearbox falls out two hundred yards down the road, I blame the mechanic.

Anyway. The project continues. Hopefully I can roll my oily sleeves up and get that chocolate bar commercial purring again by the time it reaches its airdate. We shall wait and see.

I did a train journey yesterday. (Naturally, I had to wait ages for the train.) It afforded me the rare pleasure of reading a broadsheet newspaper. In one of the articles, people with very stressful jobs were asked how they manage to remain calm. (Football Managers, A&E Doctors, Head Teachers etc.) The consensus was that having a hobby that is completely different to your job is the best antidote to stress.

Hmm. I've been working on my film in my spare time for five years now and it hasn't come out, yet. Oh well. Another few months of waiting won't hurt, especially as it's pretty common. For example, the film the editor worked on nearly a year before he cut ours is only being released later this month. And the film that recently won the BAFTA for best debut feature took three years from finished film to release. The waiting's fine, but after being so busy on the current project for so long, having nothing exciting to do or report is pretty anti-climactic. All I can say is that it's looking like being released in May or June at the mo. (Same as the chocolate bar ad!) So hopefully things will warm up again soon.

When I look back during this limbo-like period, the amount of time pressures that we worked under at certain points during the process now seem ridiculous.

Take the rehearsals, for example. You hear of stage plays, TV series(eses) and feature films having huge amounts of rehearsal time. Often you hear that directors and writers use the rehearsals to hone the script. We didn't have the time for that. Okay, we had the table read, which was helpful. But by the time we had the main cast in place, we were very near to the scheduled shoot date. The last week or so before the shoot was a blur of costume fittings, recces and the pre-production meeting.

All we had time for with the actors was a one-day read-through at the main location. Again, it was a table read. With the actors reading through their parts and a narrator there to read out the narrative parts. (*'Cut to the corridor at night. It is pitch black. A crack of light appears as a door opens slowly...'* etc etc.) It was a great moment. Finally, after four years of hearing the dialogue being played out in my head, I had the real characters in front of me bringing it all to life.

Perfect. Or nearly perfect. Only slightly ruined by the fact that the person we got in to read the narration couldn't actually read very well. I don't know where we got this person from. They weren't part of the production team. But seriously, we're talking a reading age of a nine-year-old. So what was supposed to be a serious run through of very tense scenes became an excruciating exercise in stopping myself from bursting into hysteric laughter. I couldn't make eye contact with the director, that's for sure. Or the producers. Or the actors. In fact, the stumbling over any word of three syllables or more got so bad, that I had to go to the toilet and wet myself.

When I returned, the tears wiped from my cheeks, the producers mercifully suggested a tea break. And we allowed our narrator to depart. It enabled the rest of the room to get their repressed laughter out, and served as a massive icebreaker for the production ahead.

That was a year ago. Right now, in limbo land, I've decided to use the spare time to write another screenplay. I might as well do something. My garden is low-maintenance.

I've contemplated it for several weeks and decided that, after working on a psychological thriller for so long, I will return to my natural oeuvre with the next one. It's an important step. If I am to grow as an artist, I must be true to my inner muse and let my soul speak. So a smutty comedy it is, then.

It could be the start of another five-year project. It could take longer, it could happen sooner, or it could never happen. We shall wait and see.

** The late great comedian Bill Hicks' description of the act of working in the marketing industry.*

SLIDING DOORS

FOOK. YOU KNOW THE FILM, Sliding Doors? The one where Gwyneth Paltrow, or some-such, misses a train and her life goes in two different directions? Well, even though I haven't actually seen the film, to my knowledge, I am familiar enough with its central premise to call what has happened to me today a 'Sliding Doors moment'.

Just lately, The Duchess and I have been noticing a bloke sleeping in doorways around where we live in Greenwich. We haven't been comfortable with it. Even though London has a big homeless problem, it is, by and large, a West End thing. It's something us people living or working in London get used to, I'm afraid. But we counteract our guilt by doing the right thing and buying The Big Issue every week and making standing order payments to homeless charities every month. (We all do that, don't we guys? Guys...?) Although you do get beggars and Big Issue sellers throughout the capital, actual rough sleepers in residential areas are not nearly as common.

It certainly takes the gloss off a self-satisfied saunter home from a local restaurant, warmed by fine food and alcohol, when there's a bloke shivering in a doorway at the bottom of your road.

As I sit in my living room, warmed by my roaring middle-class Swedish wood burner, I beat myself up for not waking the guy and giving him money to stay at the local backpacker's hostel for the night.

So, when a couple of weeks later on my morning stroll to the station, I see the same bloke curled up in a doorway, this time I do stop and wake him up. He sports the obligatory Catweazle beard, matted hair and filthy clothing. Although he looks ancient, when we chat I realise we are probably about the same age.

I ask him why he's sleeping rough. He says he's not homeless. He has a flat in Dartford, but he comes up this way to see his sister, but she is not always in. And as he has no money, he ends up sleeping rough sometimes.

I don't care that it sounds like a load of bollocks. I give him the contents of my pockets, which is a paltry £11.64. I also offer to buy him a train ticket to Dartford. He politely declines, saying that he prefers buses. He's quite a talker. He tells me his name is Freddy and that the reason he is in this state is that he suffers from blackouts, due to an old rugby injury. He's not a druggy. He's actually a creative in advertising. A copywriter. WHAT?

'That's what I do', I tell him. I'm a bit freaked out now.

Then he tells me that he did the same Watford advertising course as me, but two years earlier. JESUS EFFIN CHRIST. He is practically an old classmate. We were on exactly the same path. But now one of us is, literally, lying in the gutter.

I help him to his feet. A wave of astonishment, sadness and guilt washes over me. Along with the phrase 'There but for the grace of God go I'. I can think of nothing else to do but escort him to the nearest cash point. So I do. As we walk, he is chirpy as anything. He talks fondly of our course tutor, and other people in the business that we both know. I jot down my email address and give him another £60. He is made up and full of promise to be in touch. Meeting me is an amazing piece of serendipity in his eyes. It's a tragic, unsettling encounter in mine.

I jump on the train to work. I quickly e-mail ahead to say I'm running late for my first ~~argument~~ meeting of the day. Then I drop our old course tutor, Tony, a line. Telling him about the weird coincidence and asking what he knows about Freddy, and what he thinks I can do to help.

By the time I get to work, he has replied. He says, yes, he does know Freddy and his history. He says that he had a drink problem back in his college days. And that a few years after graduating, he would be hanging around Watford drinking Special Brew with the local tramps, but still saying he was working on his advertising portfolio. He says that all his classmates tried to help him, but he never admitted he had a problem. He adds that he is actually quite surprised that Freddy is still alive.

Blimey, I had been thinking of how I could maybe give him some freelance copywriting work to help him. It doesn't sound like that is appropriate. Freddy had let it slip during our chat that he once had an 8am job interview with a top advertising luminary. And he decided the best way to guarantee he would get there on time was to sleep rough in the doorway of the agency overnight.

Having that sort of logic, and a propensity to hang around with tramps in his twenties, really makes one think what kind of shit must have happened in his childhood, doesn't it?

Poor bastard. He hasn't been in touch, so far. I'm not sure how I can help him if he does. But meeting him has certainly helped me gain a bit of perspective and humility about how appreciative of my life I should be.

WHERE NAIVETY GETS YOU

I'M JUST BACK from a ten day holiday in Cornwall. It was a really fantastic break, thanks for asking. Apart from the obvious joy of getting away from it all with the missus, it was a tantalising window into the life of a proper writer.

Every day I rose early, like a proper writer. And while the Duchess slept, I sat by the window of our holiday cottage. Absorbing the scenery as I wrote for two hours solid like Ingmar Bergman probably would*. Then, when She awoke, we breakfasted well, before heading out for bracing coastal walks**. The stunning views invigorate me. And the sweet waxy aroma of the yellow flowering gorse bushes mixed with salty sea air fills my nostrils with delight, and my mind with literary delusion.

After three or so hours walking up an appetite, we would happen upon an appropriate eatery to stuff our faces with the freshest seafood imaginable, washed down with glasses of crisp white. Thence, we would repair to our rented abode overlooking a Cornish harbour where She would fire up the Kindle and I would write for a few more hours until wine o'clock. Just like Hemmingway, Orwell, or Jeffrey Archer would have done, I'm sure. Yes, I could definitely do that for a living, if I were good enough to do that for a living.

Seeing as I am not, I'm now back at work with Cornwall already a distant memory. I have ads to bash out, junior colleagues to motivate and pinheads to dance upon with strategists and clients. I also have a breakfast meeting with one of the producers of my film.

I arrive early at the ever-so-self-conscious artisan coffee shop - slash - bakery of the producer's choosing on Berwick Street. I sip a cup of rocket fuel as I wait. Watching the bearded hipster bakers removing fresh batches of bread from the oven like they invented bloody bread making. And wondering if I'm going to like the news he's going to give me on his arrival.

I am not expecting it to be great. The last couple of months have been a steep incline on the rollercoaster ride of this project. The realities of a small film trying to make a noise in a brutally money-driven industry have hit home.

Naively, I assumed that it would be a relatively straightforward procedure at this point. I was naïve. Have been from the start. I was naïve when I finished the first draft of this film five years ago and thought it was a massive achievement. I was naïve when we met the first interested producer and thought we'd cracked it. I was also naïve to think we'd cracked it when we found the right producers, then when we got the financing in place, when we casted the main actress, when we started filming, when we wrapped, when we locked the edit down and when we actually finished the film. At each milestone I was naïve enough to think that the biggest obstacle had been overcome. Each time I was wrong. Because THIS is the biggest hurdle.

We have a mountain to climb the size of the Paramount Pictures logo to convince distributors that putting our small film, made by unknowns, will attract a big audience. That there will be no empty seats, that they will earn money. Lots of money. For these people are not romantics who value artistic merit. In fact, as far as I can tell, they act as little more than a massive contrivance to service the popcorn industry. They couldn't give a shit if the film showing was the biggest load of old toss ever made, as long as it gets bums on seats. So why are they going to take a risk on giving our humble effort a chance when they can just put Gravity on for another week and get guaranteed box office takings***? The fuckers. Jesus, what good has all the money, time and effort of so many talented individuals been for, if nobody ends up seeing the finished product? It's bloody stressful. And I haven't exactly helped matters by writing forty thousand words about it in a bloody journal. Talk about setting myself up for a fall.

Blimey, this coffee is strong. I'm winding myself up here.

I calm it as the producer bounds in, full of smiles and enthusiasm and handshakes. As he chats, it becomes increasingly clear that I've been naïve once more. I hadn't bargained on the producers' levels of tenacity and creativity, it seems. They've only gone and done it! The beauties! Without being in a position to say anything too detailed right now, we have, indeed, secured a cinematic release. What's more, it's a really cool one that is not only apt for a film like ours, but also really innovative and a potential new model for independent film releases in the future. Woah.

It also seems that they found a distributer that isn't as obsessed with popcorn as they are with showing a mix of films of varying degrees of commercial appeal.

The cherry on the icing on the cake of news is that the cinema at the end of my street will be showing it. The same cinema that I have been telling my missus for years that if I ever made a film and it got shown there, I will be able to die happy.

As the meeting ends and I skip over to the editor's to recut my chocolate bar commercial for the umpteenth time, I'm buzzing. And it's only partly due to the rocket fuel coffee. With the official announcement of the official release imminent, I feel like the biggest mountain has finally been climbed. But, hey, that's naivety for you.

Geographically the furthest point in the UK from an ad agency.

** I'm writing a comedy film at the mo.*

*** On one occasion we saw the wondrous site of a school of dolphins swimming sedately in tight formation just yards from the shore. I was life-affirmed. The missus was a bit non-plussed that they didn't jump out of the water and perform backflips at all, like they do at SeaWorld. I tried my best to explain that there are no hula-hoops suspended above the waves out there. In fact, it wasn't until a day later when a local told us he'd only seen wild dolphins twice in three years that it became clear how lucky we'd been.*

**** Not that Gravity is a load of old toss, it's great, but you know what I'm saying.*

SUPER SUNDAY

IT IS THE LAST DAY of the football season today. My team - West Ham United - are away. So I'm at home watching us roll over to Man City on television.

I also have my laptop on my lap. So, as I watch our inevitable capitulation* on the telly, I am also indulging in some modern 'second screening' activity on my 'pooter. It consists of writing this instalment and simultaneously having various conversations on e-mail, text and social media.

One of them is a Facebook argument in which I am trying to reason with someone who is slagging off Liverpool fans for 'playing the victim about Hillsborough all the time'**.

The other is a Twitter conversation I manage to strike up with a famous journalist/writer/broadcaster. (He has over ninety thousand Twitter followers for Pete's sake.) He posts something on his feed about the word-length of a book he's writing. So I take the opportunity to ask him what constitutes a respectable word count for a diary-style non-fiction book.

To my surprise and admiration he posts a reply. I am already a fan of his writing, now I'm a fan of him as a man. Unfortunately, he reckons seventy thousand words is the perfect length. I do manage to negotiate him down to sixty thousand. But he adds the words 'NO LESS' in capital letters. Damn him. I was hoping he'd say fifty thousand. To date, I have written forty one thousand, eight hundred and ninety one words of this twaddle, and I was hoping that I would have enough content to get it printed and bound into a book at the end of the process.

It would, very conveniently, chalk off the 'write a book' entry on my life's 'to do' list. But I don't know if even I can string this out for another twenty thousand words.

Maybe I should go back through the whole document and get rid of all the contracted words. ~~I'm~~ I am sure ~~that'll~~ that will potentially add at least another thousand words before ~~I've~~ I have written another sentence. ~~It's~~ It is not like ~~it'll~~ it will make a huge difference. But a difference ~~nonetheless~~ none the less. And including plenty of photographs probably ~~won't~~ will not hurt much, either.

Whatever, I just want to finish it, to be honest. One, it will mean the film has come out and I can stop bothering people with this navel gazing nonsense. And two, it will serve as a handsome antidote to the day job. For it is now a full twenty months since I started a particular chocolate bar shaped advertising project and I STILL haven't got the commercial on air. I must add that this ~~isn't~~ is not typical of ad projects - ~~it's~~ it is a bit anomalous, in fact - but even so, it is a wrist slittingly painful professional experience, let me tell you.

I mean, Jesus, I have got a feature film shot, finished and distributed in the time. And, as of yesterday, I have finished a comedy feature film script, too***. ~~It's~~ It is not funny. ~~It's~~ It is going to be some sort of twisted self-flagellant achievement if I get a film, a screenplay and a book away before I manage to get this bloody commercial out. And I should know. I have 'Big' Sam Allardyce as the manager of my football team. I know all about twisted self-flagellant achievement.

** It does not matter, as we guaranteed our Premier League survival last weekend with a 2-0 home victory over Tottenham Hotspur. Our third straight victory over 'The Spurs', this season. Just saying.*

*** I'm not one for Facebook arguments. And as someone who grew up in the eighties, I am never tired of watching Liverpool lose on the pitch. But the other thing about growing up in the eighties is, I remember what it was like to watch football on over-crowded terraces, and the 'them and us' relationship between fans and Police back then. (The bloke giving it the big one on Facebook was about seven-years-old in 1989.)*

I myself was caught up in a particularly scary crush at a forth-round FA Cup tie versus QPR in 1988. It is widely acknowledged that a disaster was averted on that day, only because Loftus Road was one of the few grounds without perimeter fencing at the time. What happened to the Liverpool fans could have happened to any club. And if it had happened to another club, and the authorities had covered up who was to blame, you can be sure that the fans of that club would have fought and fought for years, noisily and relentlessly, to get justice. The 'Victim FC' thing in relation to Liverpool and Hillsborough is hateful confused nonsense. And it has to stop. So there.

**** ~~I've~~ I have just finished the first draft of my new comedy screenplay. Instead of celebrating with a single Lucky Strike cigarette, as James Caan does when he completes a manuscript in Misery, I went for the two bottles of red wine option.*

My director mate is keen to send the script out to prospective producers ~~ASAP~~ as soon as possible, but I would rather wait a while. Not for any strategic reason, other than the sooner we send it out, the sooner I will get comments back, the sooner I'll have rewrites to write. And I could do with a break.

PRE-LAUNCH

THE PUBLICITY TRAIN for the film has started rolling. The film's website is live. The poster has been launched. The Twitter and Facebook feeds are active. PR releases have been released. Actors have been lined up for interviews in national newspapers, radio and TV. The film's release dates have been announced. The trailer is out. Now is a bloody exciting time, let me tell you.

It's not exciting in the same way that actually making the film was exciting, though. It's different. At this stage, one's (and the director's) physical involvement in the process is minimal. I'm at work while this is all going on, flogging chocolate bars, train services, cooking sauces and the like. Along with the director, I feel like an expectant father, while the pregnant producers are the ones with their feet in the stirrups, sweating and cursing as they push this baby out. So the excitement is the nervous kind. Me and the director are just hanging around, not knowing quite what to do, except shout encouragement and advice from the side lines, or having the odd toke on the gas and air when no-one's looking*.

We're not really affecting very much, so we're just desperately looking forward to our baby getting out into the world, praying that the delivery is a success, so we can wet it's head and hand out cigars to all and sundry.

To push the metaphor, yet further, the birth of the film is going to be a protracted one. But protracted in a good way. We have a cinematic release scheduled for twenty-seventh of June in London, then rolling out across the country on the fifteenth of July. But before the conventional release, there's going to be a pop-up launch in Manchester. It's going to be 'Manchester's first immersive cinema experience' in fact.

It's apt. Although the film is set in London, the main character hails from Manchester. And the actress playing her lives up there, too. Also, much of the film is set high up in a city tower block. So they have converted the top floor of a city centre office block into a pop-up cinema space, so audiences will feel like they are 'a part of the action' while watching the film. And with a few other touches to make the film feel like it has 'leaked into the cinema', it should be a cool and interesting way of watching the film, I reckon**.

Already, loads of Manchester-based organs have written about it. And there's quite a bit of activity planned, like a graffiti campaign. And the film poster, designed by the same people who designed our film titles, will be wrapped around the office building that will be showing the film. There's going to be a premier, which the great and good of Manchester will hopefully attend. And me. And a regional TV news programme want to do an interview at the venue with our star actress. Hugely exciting, except that they want one of the filmmakers to do the TV interview with her. As you know, I am a ticking PR time bomb***, so it is with great pleasure and relief for myself, and the best interest of the film, that the director has agreed to conduct the interview. Phew. Cheers. It's not his natural demeanour to stand up and give it the big one in front of a camera, either. So respect due to him. Maybe I should go up to Manchester with him for the day and ~~heckle him~~ lend him my moral support.

Another big promotional tool just released is the teaser trailer. It's not the full trailer yet (that will be released nearer the London launch, I think). It's only a minute long. But I like it, because it manages to be pretty gripping, but without giving anything of the plot away. Hopefully, the people who have seen it and liked it aren't just being polite. I swear I'm not lying when I say I had nothing to do with cutting it together. My step-daughter only appearing as an extra for five seconds of a ninety-three-minute film, yet still managing to get her scowling face into the bloody trailer is pure coincidence. Honest.

Meanwhile, whoever it is who is running the film's social media feeds is getting busy, forwarding, tweeting and posting all the trailer, article, ticket info etc. etc. at regular intervals. In turn, I've been clogging up my Facebook and Twitter feeds inviting my friends to like and follow those pages, re-tweeting and sharing all sorts of updates. I recognise that this is all a bit much. I hereby apologise to all my social media friends for this relentless self-promotion. Sorry. I really can't help myself. It's such a big deal to me. I am like an excited, expectant parent posting multiple pictures of baby scans, the spare room I've just converted into a nursery, the cot I've just assembled, my partner's ever-expanding belly etc. Which, when I put it like that, makes it pretty standard on-line behaviour. But sorry, anyway.

* *Me and the missus went to a 21st birthday party a couple of weeks back. (Our friends' daughter's 21st.) It was a BBQ, with mucho vino. I had a lovely time. And so much vin rouge, that when the youngsters started inhaling balloons - the latest party drug craze - I thought it was a really good idea to join in. (Basically, all 'da kids' these days are getting off on inhaling balloons full of nitrous oxide, the same gas that is the 'gas' of 'gas and air' in hospital delivery rooms. For more information, ask someone in their twenties.)*

Anyway, I did a balloon. And after buzzing my tits off and dancing like Ian Curtis for five minutes, I felt a bit 'odd'. So the missus bundled me into a car. I crashed out for the whole journey then chucked my guts up really violently when I got back home. I blame the wine.

** *I am so excited, I didn't even allow myself to be too annoyed when the launch date was put back a week because Manchester council dragged their heels in granting our pop-up venue a liquor licence. Thereby losing me and the missus and our friends the cost of our non-transferable train tickets. I blame the wine (licence).*

*** *My impressive PR credentials are outlined in the chapter entitled 'Interrogation'.*

PREMIER MOVIE TENSION

I'M SITTING ON A VIRGIN train as I write. It's an appropriate de-nationalised franchise, as this journey is a whole new experience for me. The missus and I are on our way up to Manchester to attend the premier of my film. Sorry, I'm just going to write that again. The missus and I are on our way up to Manchester to attend the premier of my film. Bloody fucking Nora, that's probably the best sentence I've ever written. I never thought I'd actually get to write that, you know. Not in a non-fiction piece, anyway.

What's odder is that at the moment I type and retype it, the train flashes past the town of Watford. The town where I actually started on this meandering non-thought-out path that somehow ended up with me on this train. Watford College (or West Herts College as it is officially titled) is anomalous amongst the colleges of non-descript satellite towns in that it happens to host the foremost creative ad course in the UK, arguably the world. Weird, but true*.

Twenty years ago I was languishing on a Business Studies HND course at UWE Bristol. There was a marketing element to the course and every now and again this old copywriter bloke –

called Terry – used to come in and take seminars about advertising. And he used to set us creative briefs, too. Amazingly, he and I got on. Unlike all the other lecturers, he actually seemed to like my piss-taking, wise-arse attitude in lessons. He said to me that I was wasting my time doing business studies, and suggested that I apply for the Advertising Copywriting & Art Direction course in Watford. Growing up in the nearby town of Welwyn Garden City, the thought of relocating from the vibrant cultured city of Bristol to a shitty Hertfordshire town felt like rather a big step backwards. But it was more than made up for by the prospect of doing a course involving feet on desks, thinking up stupid ideas all day long and the chance of a job at the end of it that didn't include wearing a suit.

I applied. Did a copy test. Did an interview, and got in. And the rest, as they say, is not at all interesting. But I am nevertheless enjoying sitting back on the train and having time to relax and reflect. It's been a tough few days at the office, cramming five days of work into three.

It's also been bloody hard to concentrate on the jobs in hand with media noise ringing in my ears. Our BLA (brilliant lead actress) has been doing a few radio interviews to plug us. She was on BBC Radio 5Live on Tuesday. National radio, baby! I was so excited that I took the hugely unprofessional step of declining a client conference call at short notice in order to listen to the show.

On Wednesday I was so busy preparing a client presentation that I missed her talking about the film on BBC Radio 6 Music. Gutted! And I also missed her interview on BBC Radio Manchester. In it, she actually likened me to other writers she has worked with, including Victoria Wood, Paul Abbot and Peter Moffat!!

Fookin' 'ell! Talk about surreal! Amazing generosity!

However, before I can get too drunk on it, my old advertising creative partner from Watford College hastens to remind me on Facebook that I look nothing like Victoria Wood. It's a fair point. And the knowledge that I was almost certainly the only one of said writers who was in a meeting about cooking sauce while the interview aired, also helps the sobriety.

I could do with a drink right now, however. As we pull into Manchester Piccadilly Station, the butterflies in my stomach start to flap. Blimey. This is an odd feeling. I actually feel a bit unwell on it. I desperately hope it goes well tonight. I hope that my Dad and Step-Mum enjoy themselves. And behave themselves. I hope it's not an anti-climax for my mate from Manchester after hearing me banging on about it for so long. I hope the press like it. Or don't hate it, at least. And I hope and pray that the director has fallen for my wind-up that tonight's dress code is dinner suits and dickie-bows. Please God, let it all go well.

* *I've mentioned my college and course tutor before in the 'Sliding Doors' chapter. Watford has a great advertising course due to the fact that the town was built on its printing and paper production industry. It followed that the local college specialised in complimentary courses like publishing, typography and advertising*

Even though Watford is no longer a printing town, it still knocks out advertising creative talent that work and run the best ad creative departments in the world. (Including my boss. He's younger, better looking, and graduated two years after me, which pisses me off rather.)

The course tutor is a slightly eccentric, loveable, advertising and football-obsessed bloke called Tony Cullingham. He has run the course for more than twenty-five years now. In that time, supplying literally hundreds of top creative professionals into the industry with his unique brand of inspiration, brutal criticism, paternal encouragement and Friday lunchtime kick-abouts. I think he deserves just as many plaudits for services to advertising as Sir John Hegarty. (An ad legend and former boss of mine.) Tony teaches his students how to think rigorously, take criticism lightly, act professionally, and apply ideas universally. That's why so many of his charges have not only blazed a trail through ad land but created a stir in other creative industries too. (Just off the top of my head, I can think of old Watfordians who are in TV, Film, Novels, Comedy, Fashion, Fine Art, Illustration, Teaching, Furniture Design, Product Innovation, Greetings Cards and Children's Books. Oh, and Savoury Snacks Innovations!)

Tony is an amazing teacher. But dedicated as he is, I know for certain that he would give it all up, along with his left testicle, to run out just once in the colours of Leicester City FC.

PART FIVE
RELEASE

WORLD PREMIER

I AM FEELING BLOODY ODD. Have done all afternoon. We've found and checked in to the apartment we've rented for the weekend. We've nipped out to Manchester's shopping district and bought me a new pair of trainers for tonight. It was a panic buy. Even as I walked out of the shop I admit to the missus that they are at least ten years too young for me. We stroll back to the apartment, via the Co-op for bread, milk, and booze. I take in the magnificent vista from the balcony of the back of Aldi supermarket. My phone is buzzing off the hook with texts, e-mails, tweets and posts from mates wishing me well and colleagues wishing me total and utter failure. (In the most endearing possible way, of course.) (I think.)

Despite the excitement, it has the opposite effect on me and I end up snoozing on the sofa for the last hour before I have to leave. It's a quick tactical kip. And it does the trick, with the help of a sugar free Red Bull. But I still feel a bit odd. I'm not nervous in particular, but maybe I am. Oh, I dunno. I shower, dress myself in my version of smart (basically, the same stuff I always wear, but box fresh versions of them), and then head out.

The director has found what he describes as an 'all right, as it goes' Chinese restaurant in Chinatown for us to meet and line our stomachs. (I say Chinatown. China-half-a-street would be more accurate.) As the missus and I enter the restaurant, full of expectation, we are confronted by the first disaster of the evening. The director is dressed in the same 'smart/scruffy' attire as myself, not the dinner suit that I had tried my best to mislead him into wearing. Damn. And what's more, he immediately spots my colourful footwear and likens them to something out of Timmy Mallet's wardrobe. Double damn. I hope it's not an indicator of how the rest of the night is going to go.

At least the food is tasty, fast and cheap. We bolt it and nip around the corner to a little boozer where our (hugely talented and lovely) second leading actress is plotted-up with all her actor, musician and broadcast friends that she's invited to the premier. It's like a creative who's who of Manchester in here. And luckily someone has just got a round in, so I get off quite lightly at the bar. The night is looking up.

Again, we can't hang about. We have agreed to meet our Manchester mate, Leslie and my Dad and Step-Mum at the venue at seven. My dad is a bit of a mentalist when it comes to punctuality. (Are all parents like that?) So we 'sup up' as they say 'oop t'north' and nip across to the venue.

I round the corner to the tower block, whose top floor has been converted into a cinema space, and - BOSH! – I am hit straight in the face by the hugest poster I have ever seen. It's our film poster. It runs three stories high and the entire width of the building. It looks fucking amazing. It does to me, anyway. No, sod it. It looks fucking amazing, full stop. A rush of adrenaline courses through me. My head is spinning slightly at the amount of things bombarding me at the same time. I'm trying to take in the magnificence of the greatest poster I've ever had run, while simultaneously greeting my friend, greeting one of the producers, helping my dad and step-mum step out of a cab, noticing that my father has, indeed, bitten on the dinner suit joke, getting my picture taken by a photographer and getting ushered inside to be interviewed by the Manchester Evening News. Before I know it, I'm talking shit to a journalist. As the stuff's coming out of my mouth I immediately haven't got a clue what I've just said, but nevertheless, she scribbles it down in shorthand. (Shorthand! They actually still do that.) Then it's up in the lift to the top floor for more greetings, small talk and nervous sips of champagne.

My dad looks fantastic in his dickie bow. It's brilliant to have my better half, family and friends here. Special. But I feel weird. It's like I'm here, but not. A spectator. I reckon the events unfolding around me are so surreal to me that my tiny little head cannot quite compute it.

When the champagne reception is done and it's time for the special guests to take their seats, I usher my loved ones to the front but hang back, myself. The director, co-starring actress and myself edge out of the room, but the producer stops and asks us to watch. The director and I oblige, but the actress legs it. (She doesn't like watching herself. Fair dos.)

We perch at the back, nervously. He and I have had absolutely no involvement in the 'immersive cinema' elements of the pop-up launch**, so the event is almost as fresh an experience for us as it is for the rest of the audience. Despite our nervousness, I have to say that they have done a fantastic job in making the movie become a compelling '4D experience'*** every seat has an iPad and headphones attached, which sends viewers the sound of the film through an app. Oh yeah, it's pretty techno. I watch the audience reactions more than the film. When our BLA (brilliant leading actress) sneaks in to the back of the room near the end of the film (she's been filming all day, so could only arrive late), the director and I remove our headphones to greet her. Thereby having the satisfying experience of hearing the entire audience gasp and scream in horror at the film's final denouement****.

Whoosh. The sound washes over me like a euphoric wave.

The titles appear.

The audience applauds.

I'm flying as the elevator takes me down to terra firma. I take in the final theatrical touch of the night's immersive performance.

I take a photograph of the two actresses standing in front of the huge poster.

I repair to the trendy bar for the after-party.

I prop up the bar with my old man and the director.

I meet and drink and talk about the film with several famous actors, radio broadcasters, journalists, musicians, rock stars and parents of brilliant leading actresses.

I stagger home, pissed, at three a.m.

I sit down.

I kick off my Timmy Mallets.

I sigh.

I think, 'Did all that just happen?'

**Apart from some sound design elements to be played in the elevator as audiences ascend to the top floor. Courtesy of Tim, the sound engineer at work. Cheers, Tim!*

*** A '4D experience' is how immersive cinema is described. I didn't coin the phrase, okay? So don't blame me. But whatever you call it, the producers have done fantastically well. For a start, hosting it on the top of a tower block – with imperious views of the city to mirror the settings of the film – is inspired. And from the moment you arrive at the front door before the film to when you leave the building at the end, they have used actors, props, sound effects and even the choice of refreshments to 'leak' the film into the audience's world. I think it's great. And I'm a cynical sod.*

**** Yes, I just used the word 'denouement'. Got a problem with that? You have? Well, deal with it; I'm a screenwriter now. We chuck pretentious words and phrases around like so much confetti. That's our raison d'etre.*

INTERMISSION

THIS WEEK I AM having a break from the excitement of my film's Manchester release. A lot's been going on since the premier. The regional press up there has reviewed the film, as have several film websites. It's been nerve-wracking waiting for the critics' judgment. And being that the Manchester release is a pop-up 4D one, the anxiety is doubled. Because the critics are not just judging the film, they are judging the whole experience.

But get this: they like it! Sweet baby Jesus and the angels from above, they like it. I can't tell you how wonderful that is. It feels like a lottery win. But better.

It's also quite odd. When working on the script I spent an unhealthy amount of time thinking hard about every aspect of the story. (But not overthinking!) As deeply as myself and the director immersed ourselves, it is now over a year since we last thought about the meanings and themes of the film.

Even when we were in production and post-production, we were thinking about the minutiae, not the bigger picture of the picture. And when I watch the film now, I'm looking at it technically, rather than as a story.

Also, I've written a whole new film since this one was finished. And with all the stuff going on at work, I have to admit that I have kind of forgotten quite a lot of the depth in the story. So, yeah, it's odd to have the text and subtext of it played back to me. And hugely satisfying (dare I say emotional?) that none of the subtleties we thought hard about have been lost on people.

Yes, it's such an exciting time. I feel embarrassed about the amount of self-congratulatory stuff I'm posting on social media at the moment.

'Yeah, but not embarrassed enough to not do it, you twat' I hear you retort. It's a fair cop.

So it's good (for all concerned) that I am removing myself from this self-congratulatory bubble this week. Unfortunately, it's a leap from a self-congratulatory frying pan into a self-congratulatory fire, as I am flying out to attend the Cannes Festival. No, not the film one. the advertising one.

With the greatest respect to the advertising industry, it is fair to say that it is the poor relation of the Cannes festivals. It doesn't have the superstars of its movie counterpart. Well, it does have stars, although you would have only heard of them if you work in advertising. I'm talking about the star advertising practitioners, of course. The people who think up the ads*, not the actors/characters in the ads themselves. It's a shame, because it would be bloody funny if it was all about The Honey Monster, Ronald McDonald, Mister Muscle etc. giving it large on the red carpet. And having a coke and hooker fest at the after party. I bet Hamburgler and Homepride Fred are a right couple of deviant bastards when they get going. Watch out Special K Girl. They'll have that red swimming costume down by your ankles before you can say 'fortified with vitamins and iron'.

But, no, the advertising festival isn't as glittery as the film festival, but it's still in Cannes. The sky is still perfectly azure, the beaches are still thronging with the beautiful and the hotels are still just as opulent.

I hope, I really really hope, that at some point in my life I will get to compare the two Cannes festivals, first hand. But right now I can only assume that the giants of the film industry who flock to Cannes at the end of May use the week as a chance to live it up in expensive hotels, posh villas, or flash yachts, attending as many free parties as they can possibly fit in, gorge themselves on the finest wine, drugs, cigars, and cuisine that money can buy and generally revel in their own excess and ridiculousness like a snake that's swallowed a hippo.

At the ad festival, the crème de la crème of the advertising wankers of the world do their very best to be as decadent and vulgar as is humanly possible.

The epicentre of this vulgarity is the Terrace Bar at the Carlton Hotel (although The Gutter Bar** in the shadow of the Hotel Martinez gives it a good run for its Euro). I definitely can't think of another gaff I've ever drunk in where the standard drink order is a jeroboam of rose wine. And that said drink order is about €300 a pop. Even a small beer is €12 FFS***.

Oh yeah, Cannes sees us advertising types coming, all right. Apparently, the price of everything in the town ramps up to its highest for the week of the ad festival. Just as production and post-production companies charge a premium for commercial work over other broadcast jobs, so too does a conference town (Cannes is essentially a conference town, albeit a bloody glamorous one.)

So the owners of the flash yachts and sumptuous holiday villas of the town are able to rent them out to ad people for the week at a considerably higher rate than even the film companies would be charged the month previous.

Having said that, it's actually one of the cheapest weeks on the piss I'm ever likely to have****. Everywhere I go it's either a free party thrown by an agency, production company etc. or there's a kindly rep from some production company or other on hand to pick up the tab. In fact, there are so many free parties in the bars, beaches or villas during the week that they publish a timetable of events, so you can plan your ligging to maximum effect. In turn, each company tries its best to make their bash the coolest and most exclusive of the week.

I wear four or five of those brightly coloured festival-style wristbands all week for various parties that I don't even end up attending. And I have to blag my way into a few parties that I'm not on the guest list for, too. One is a barbeque at a sumptuous hillside villa, thrown by a Chinese production company. Not only had I not heard of the company, I was not invited. But I tagged along with my drunken northern mates, anyway, as they assured me they could 'blag me in'.

We make it to the villa in a cab ride paid for by a production company rep. I give my assumed name to get into the party*****. The guest list dude asks me how to spell it. I get half way through spelling my assumed surname when my mate steps in and says,

'Hey 'Rick', that's not how you spell it. You spell it like this...'

Incredibly, I am allowed in. And we proceed to throw as much barbequed food and free beer down our necks as possible. All the while laughing at the eurotrash by the side of the pool in their speedos who are dancing (and gurning) to the eurotrance crap that the DJ is serving up. It's three in the afternoon, FFS!

It's a fun party in an idyllic setting. But as soon as the beer runs out, so do we. And it is only then that we realise the speedo gurners are, in fact, English.

FFS.

My digs for the week is a luxury apartment in the centre of the town. It is a beautiful, spacious and modern five-bedroom place that I'm sharing with my bosses and a couple of others from the agency. The place quickly assumes the feel of a forty-something version of a student flat. A mix of dirty dishes, six a.m. drinking and lots of piss take and banter. As an agency representative, I attend a couple of dinners with my colleagues, a lecture or two, a fancy cocktail party with the worldwide American bosses of the agency network we are part of, and a stuffy drink and chat with some industry journalists. But apart from that, I spend most of my time bumping into old mukkas I have previously worked with and talk a lot of drunken shit.

The awards that are given out at the festival are metal sculptures in the shape of a lion. I had joked to my colleagues in the office that I would be wearing a t-shirt all week with the legend 'movie beats lion' emblazoned across the chest. I don't, but nevertheless it is written right across my punch-able face as I catch up with people.

And after several relentless days of this horrific hilariousness, I am more than ready to get home for a restful weekend. I need it. As next week it's the film's London premier and London release. One's drinking trousers will need to be fully laundered and ironed for that.

**One of the ridiculous things about advertising is that it has its own stars. These are the people who exist in the firmament, earning out-of-this-world kind of money, with their names above the door of the agency they run. And everything they touch seemingly turning to gold. It's crazy, but it's also fantastic. Because advertising is a hugely meritocratic (and non-sexist) industry that allows any young person to quickly improve their salary on the strength of their work. And it only takes one amazing piece of work to achieve it. That's why there are so many agencies with creative heads in their early thirties.*

I'm not one of the people who have managed to make a career-defining ad. That's why my bosses are younger than me. And probably why I'm so cynical. (Or is it because I'm so cynical that I'm not running my own agency? Dunno. Actually, it's probably cos I'm a bit shit.)

*** Interesting fact. In the film world, they don't call The Gutter Bar, The Gutter Bar. They call it Le Petit Martinez. Okay, not too interesting a fact, but a fact, nonetheless.*

**** One evening I bump into some student ad creatives who have recently completed an internship at my agency. They are here because they are up for the student award. They won! But they are here on their own steam, so I offer to buy them a pizza and a beer as a celebratory gesture. All good, but when it came to going for more drinks afterwards, even my expenses couldn't justify spending several hundred Euros on 'drinks at Carlton Terrace with students'.*

*****There are two types of people at the Cannes ad festival. Those who are up for an award and those who aren't. The ones that are, are keen to immerse themselves in the creativity on show, attend all the ceremonies and talk about the work. They are excited beyond belief, because they know that if they win they will receive a huge metal doorstop in the shape of a lion and noughts on their salary. Those that aren't up for an award have absolutely no interest in the work and are unashamedly there to get as much free booze and networking done as they possibly can. In fact, so good is the potential for free partying, some people in advertising, take the week off as holiday and fly down for cheap sunny excess.*

I'm in the 'only here for the party' section. Despite an international press campaign that I wrote being hotly tipped for award success, the client wouldn't let us enter the work into the competition. (Politics. Don't ask.)

****** It's the nearest I've ever been to wining the Cannes Grand Prix for the best ad in the world. The bloke whose name I assumed to get into the party won the Grand Prix at the end of the week. Note to self - become friends with him as he will be running his own ad agency (and shitting pound notes) in no time.*

LONDON PREMIER

TWO PREMIERES MIGHT SEEM a little excessive, but as someone who has divorced parents it's a bloody godsend. It's a hot day. At six p.m. the sun still thinks it's mid-afternoon. Lovely, but a little uncomfortable and not particularly conducive to a night at the cinema. It's proper Betty Swollocks weather in fact, as I walk from the agency to Kings Cross Station to meet my 'plus one' for the evening, my Mum.

Unfortunately, the chip in my bankcard has decided to stop working. I have no cash. So my first act after hugging and kissing dearest ma-ma at our point of rendezvous - Pret A Manger dans le concourse de la Gare de Roi Croix - is to tap her up for a oner.

We jump a Hackney cab to Hackney (my treat now I'm flush). Not Leicester Square. Picturehouse being an independent chain, they don't bother having a ridiculously overpriced West End theatre. Good. It means they have lower overheads and can, therefore, put on more low budget independent films. So power to them. Eff the multiplex. And hooray for Hackney.

We arrive.

Flash bulbs do not go off.

I hug and kiss producers at the doorway.

Flash bulbs go off.

We turn to see our leading male actor striding towards the cinema with his missus. More hugs and kisses. I then head into the bar to find my mate, Lee*, who is my 'plus two' this evening. Here, I also find the director and his family, and the supporting lead actress. More hugs and kisses.

Everyone's here, except the BLA (brilliant leading actress) herself. She's filming the second series of a BBC drama up north, so is probably knee deep in Yorkshire mud in her period costume while we are sipping our drinks.

I am nowhere near as nervous as I was in Manchester. Still quite nervous, but I don't feel physically unwell, which is an improvement. However, due to the midsummer temperatures, and no doubt the stone of timber I'm carrying at the moment (alright, two stones), I've got a bit of a sweat on.

We're ushered upstairs to an area with a red carpet and film-branded backdrop for film premier photographic opportunities.

The producers and the actors know the drill and are soon being snapped in various front hip forward, tummy in, chin up poses. The director and I sheepishly mill around chatting to our guests (including my step-daughter, who is my 'plus three' for the evening). And as the photographers haven't got a Danny Le Rue who the hell we are, we don't actually end up getting our photos taken properly. But I do get a couple of phone snaps of me and my mum, and me and my daughter, which is good enough for me.

Screen one of Hackney Picturehouse is humongous, by the way. The banking of the two hundred and forty-odd seats is really steep, so the screen is basically the whole front wall of the theatre.

It's almost Imax-like in it's scale. As we file in and take our seats, we notice a huge still of our film poster filling the screen. Yes!

The lights dim. The producers take the stage to say a few words in the spotlight. They invite the director and writer onto the stage. No!

I stand next to the director. He's 6'5". I look like a fat sweating dwarf in comparison. Nice!

They invite the actors onto stage. Safety in numbers. People are introduced, thanked and clapped. Then it's back to our seats to sit through the film. It plays out pretty well. The audience gasp, snigger and shriek in all the right places. Even though my mum was at the rough cut screening at BAFTA, she still screams at the end. (Admittedly it was over a year ago, but still.)

The after-party is in a private bar in the cinema. My mum immediately notices the smattering of well-known actors that are here. She eschews the nibbles (but not the free wine) and makes sure she introduces herself to them as 'Writer's Mother'. It must be writer's mother's prerogative to be forward in these situations, because the actors seem more than happy to chat with her and give her a kiss.

When I put her in a cab later she is positively glowing. And it's not entirely down to the free wine. As I skip back to the party I'm glowing. Proud that she's proud.

I too pretty much eschew the nibbles and concentrate on the booze. And proceed to talk emotional drunk talk with my mate, my daughter, the director, the actors, the producers, other technicians, and actor friends of the actors. Basically, anyone who is there gets the dubious benefit of my drunk emotional ramblings.

Christ knows what time we get kicked out, but the last thing I remember is sitting at a bus stop swigging a bottle of beer, keeping the associate producer company while she waits for her night bus. And the next thing, I'm waking up outside my front door and shoving a ridiculous amount of cash for a seven-mile journey into the hand of a cab driver. (It's not like he's had to row me across the river. There's a tunnel, FFS.)

After waking up the missus to be let into the house because I've left my key at work, I sink into bed. What a fantastic night.

**Lee is the man who suggested I write down my filmmaking experiences. So blame him for this drivel.*

CRITICS

MY HEAD HURTS. Last night was a cracker, but I'm feeling it right now. Thank the Lord I booked the day off work today. Not that it's a tactical duvet day. But still - result. I can at least relax this morning until our houseguests arrive at around lunchtime.

We're throwing a 'Shit the bed! I've got a movie released!' party tomorrow night. So my cousin and his wife will be staying with us for the weekend. Actually, I can't relax. At all. Today is the day that most of the movie reviews of the film come out.

So as well as a hangover, I have a shitloads of nerves to contend with. The regional reviews may have been kind, but it's the national ones that count. Big movies attract big audiences by their sheer scale, the magnitude of their cast, the weight of publicity surrounding their release and the critics' reviews. Independent films on the other hand, rely almost entirely on favourable reviews to attract an audience. So, what the critics say is really important to the film's success. And besides, who doesn't want people who are paid to have an opinion to have a favourable opinion of their work? I certainly do.

These opinions start coming in immediately. As soon as I wake up I remember a text I received last night from our BLA (brilliant lead actress), saying how good the review had been on that evening's BBC Radio 4 Front Row review program. I find it online. It's great. Mark Eccleston, BBC (and Sky News) film critic says that our BLA *'is absolutely terrific, in a very good film that punches above its weight"*

Yes! He even mentions me by name! Okay, he pronounces my name incorrectly, but sod it, I'm being talked about on national radio by a respected film person! Woohoo!

The only odd thing is that the female presenter comments that, as a feminist, she didn't like the way the film presents an idea that women can only achieve happiness with a traditional lifestyle*. That's a bit odd. Blimey. Throughout the whole five-year process, which has included many very strong and impressive women in key positions that have never once been raised as an issue. (Three of the four main actors, the production designer, and the producer of the film are just some of the strong women on the project.) And it certainly wasn't our intention to make such a point. It's a psychological thriller we've made, not a sociological thriller!

Luckily, Eccleston argues successfully in response that, on the contrary, a film with strong working class northern women in the lead roles is something not seen on the big screen since the likes of Rita Tushingham in the kitchen sink dramas of the 1960's. So, slightly left-field criticism aside, it's a great review. I'd certainly seek out the film on the strength of that recommendation, if I were a punter.

It propels me to the shower. And helps the hangover diminish. Then, over tea and toast, I pour over the newspaper reviews.

With every one I read, my spirits either soar or plummet. I hate the phrase 'rollercoaster of emotion' but that's exactly what I'm on.

One minute I'm doing a loop the loop while reading the Daily Star describe it as *'a stylish film... packed with some very big surprises'.* (Outtake - Go see this movie.)

Five minutes later I'm almost regurgitating breakfast as I plummet earthwards while reading the Guardian's Leslie Felperin (no, I've never heard of her, either) dismiss it as '*a thriller with diminishing returns*'. (Outtake – don't watch this movie.)

Then I am moonwalking in the firmament as I read Brian Viner in The Mail (I have heard of him) pronounce it *'a taut, well-crafted thriller'.* Boom! (Outtake - Go and see this movie.)

Then I crash land in an emotional heap when I read Kate Muir in The Times describe it as '*mediocre*'. (Outtake – don't go and watch this movie.)

And I'm not sure how to feel about Geoffrey MacNab's assessment in The Independent that: '*Bold British Thriller's originality lies in unsympathetic lead character... this makes it hard to root for her or to warm to the film in spite of the grimly effective way in which it is constructed*'. (Outtake – dunno whether to watch this movie, or not.)

Blimey. I feel like I'm blinking bi-polar. I'm so preoccupied with the cartoon bluebirds flying around my head that my missus (who also has the day off) gives up trying to have a conversation with me.

Every negative written word is like a knife in my guts. Every positive comment is a euphoric affirmation. The hangover has gone, but my head hurts as I tune in to BBC Radio 5 Live for the Kermode and Mayo film review show. This is an important one. Not only is it a hugely popular Friday lunchtime live broadcast, it's also 'the biggest film review podcast in the world'. It's Mark Kermode, man! He of the 1950s Brylcreme hair. He of TV, radio, broadsheet newspapers and bestselling film books fame. He's the most famous practicing film critic in the UK, no less. Out of all of them, he is the one I really would like to impress.

I listen intently. It's a two-hour show. I know he's been sent the film to watch, but I don't know when, if at all, he is going to discuss it on air. After what seems like hours, but probably thirty minutes, he does.

My missus, who's repaired upstairs to get away from me, later describes hearing 'a sudden strangulated, urgent yelp from downstairs, like you'd caught yourself in your zip' when she hears me react to Mark Kermode telling the nation my film's *"a taut, slightly nasty story, well told and well played."*

He likes it! Admittedly, he's not doing a cartwheel about it. But I am! He bloody fucking likes it. Do you hear that Kate Muir of The Times? Do you?! The Kermode likes it! Yes, whatever-your-name-is from The Guardian - He likes it. He even mentions me by name! Okay, he pronounces my name incorrectly, but sod it; I'm being talked about on national radio by a respected film person! For the second time in twenty-four hours!

Despite the elation of hearing people I respect say nice things about my work, I can't quite shake the negative comments from my mind. I can suddenly see why they say never read your own reviews. It's not like you can only take on board the ones you agree with and dismiss the ones you don't. You have to take it all on the chin(s). And/or try not to take it personally, or seriously. They are just opinions, after all. Often widely different to each other. Although, I do note that with every single review, whether positive or negative about the film in general, there's a consensus that our BLA (brilliant lead actress) is, indeed, brilliant.

Today has been another experience to add to the list of amazing things that have happened to me recently. It has been a brutal and exciting ride. I've spent almost twenty years having my work judged, critiqued and awarded (or not) in advertising. But this is taking the idea of 'sticking your head above the parapet' to a whole new level. It's hateful and beautiful at the same time. And it shatters one's nerves.

All I know for certain is, I do not possess the negative energy required to be a critic.

By the time I've finished an excited phone conversation with the director about the morning's events, I am actually pretty bloody shattered****. Emotionally, that is. My time for quiet reflection and navel gazing is fleeting, however, as my cousins promptly arrive with an off licence worth of booze and a thirst on. And before I know it, I'm getting on it again.

** This line of criticism is leveled at the film more than once. I think the fact that it is written and directed by two blokes has made some people over-scrutinize the character. (The 'female character written/directed by two blokes' thing was even articulated a couple of times in reviews.) Trust me, our BLA (brilliant lead actress) and fantastic supporting female actress would not have touched this film with a barge pole if they thought for a nanosecond that it was at all derogatory to women. In fact, they were attracted to the project because of the strong depiction of women.*

So there.

It's funny what critics pick up on. In one really positive review, the critic picked up on one tiny detail – the fact that the building in which the main character lives is called Elysium Heights – and proceeded to liken the whole film to Greek tragedy. Fair play, except the fact that the name wasn't anything that was written specifically into the film. The art director had to change the livery of the building when filming and Elysium was just one of his suggestions that we picked.

Even funnier, Charlotte O'Sullivan in The London Evening Standard uses her review to tell all her readers that she didn't want to like the main character because she employs a cleaner in the film. 'I'm not a fan of people who have "staff" (why can't people clean up their own mess?)'.

Bloody hell.

*** The director has been through the exact same emotional theme park ride as myself.*

PARTY TIME

CAN HANGOVERS BE CUMULATIVE? It feels like they can. I have been on the piss pretty much constantly for a whole month now. (Manchester prem, Cannes ad festival, London premier, and loads more in between.) I feel like a slug. Last night was my fifth night out in a row. Even at my drinking peak in my early twenties student days, I would be melting after five nights out in a row. I would not have been so tubby, but I would have been feeling just as shit.

I say I'm feeling shit. I mean physically. Mentally, I am soaring like an eagle, what with all the wonderful things happening at the moment. So, despite my organs begging me for a rest, I am raring to make it six in a row.

Tonight is the big one. I told you that my ambition was to go and see my own film on a Saturday night at the cinema at the end of my street. Well, tonight I'm going to fulfill that ambition. And I've invited my friends and family to join me.

One hundred and thirty people in total.

I know, I didn't think I was that popular, either.

All I can say is, having a supportive family and a very popular missus helps swell the numbers.

Seeing as people are descending on us from such far-flung exotic locations as Milton Keynes, Gloucestershire, Cambridge, Portsmouth and Glasgow, me and the missus decide to spend our money on throwing a proper after-party. Therefore, being that it's a public showing, we ask people to buy their own cinema tickets.

This is actually more complicated than it sounds. In order to make this happen, I have to get in touch with the head office of Picturehouse cinemas and ask them kindly if they could put on a showing at a certain time on a Saturday in a certain screen that would hold all of my people. (Screen two, six-thirty p.m. This means we'll be out of the cinema by eight-fifteen. Any later and we'd be cutting into valuable drinking time at the after-party.) In order for this to happen, Picturehouse open a link on their website, so my people can purchase their tickets before the general public.

It goes really well. So well, in fact, that the cinema manager calls me three days before the show to ask if I would mind if they bumped the performance from screen two to screen one - a one hundred and eighty seater?

Obviously, I 'umm' and 'ahh' for the best part of a tenth of a second before agreeing, and reassure him that my mates are a friendly, non-litigious bunch who won't kick off about the screen and seat numbers on their tickets no longer being valid. Woohoo.

Where yesterday I was preoccupied with all the review stuff flying about, today feels like a weight has been lifted from my shoulders. I'm not at all nervous about tonight. My mates aren't going to slag the film off to my face, even if they don't like it.

I hope.

And besides, a fair proportion of them came to the rough cut screening a year ago. So they know what's in store.

I spend the day hanging in the garden, mostly, with our house guests and other early arriving mates, trying my best not to start drinking too early. Without success.

All too quickly, it's knocking on five-thirty. I told everyone I'd be in the cinema bar from five forty-five and I haven't even been down to the party venue to decorate it, yet. So I leave the missus and guests to it and leg it down there. I've printed out a load of screen grabs from the scene in the film where my lot appear as extras. I stick them up all around the venue along with a load of film posters.

That done, I leg it back for a quick S, S and S, then stroll down the road as calmly as possible to the cinema.

I am met with the fantastic sight of all my favourite people in the world in one place. What follows is a wonderful blur of bear hugs, kisses and backslaps, and the drinking of one pint, before we are ushered into screen one.

Amazingly, it is a sell out. (I know this because one of my step-daughter's late arriving friend couldn't get a ticket and we had to blag him in to sit in the place of another friend who couldn't make it because his kid was ill.) That means there are fifty genuine punters in the room, too! It means my local ad campaign must have worked*. And it also means that, as the last one in, I have to sit right at the front. Not a problem. I've seen it. But I'd rather have sat right at the back with the director and been able to take in the reactions of the room as the film unfolds.

It would also have saved me having to sink in my seat with tears in my eyes when the film ends.

The fifty ordinary punters (all possessors of exquisite taste and discernment) must wonder what the heck is going on when everyone starts clapping and then the cheering when the writer credit appears on screen.

It is an incredible feeling. Like scoring the winner in front of your own fans. Something I will never forget.

The rest of the night, however, goes by in a complete blur. I lead our guests down the street, pied-piper-like, to the basement bar we've hired. And proceed to drink, talk bollocks and make a tit of myself on the dance floor until the early hours.

Christ knows what goes on, but I have a lovely time surrounded by lovely people.

Rumour has it, at one point during the night a pissed slug of a man attempts to show the youngsters at the party the amazing breakdancing moves he learned as a ten-year-old back in 1983. Unfortunately, there is no photographic or video evidence to back it up, however.

** A week ago I printed out some A4 sized film posters with 'written by a local resident' on them and asked a few of the shops down my street to put them in their windows. The bloke in the greengrocers, who has known me for all of the eight years I've lived on the street, couldn't believe it. As, for all that time, he had assumed I was a builder or some such. A builder? With these silky soft hands? (I actually took it as a bit of compliment, as it goes, being the son of a carpenter, an' all.*

GENERAL RELEASE

I'VE BEEN TO THE PICTURES quite a lot in the last couple of weeks. Well, you've got to, haven't you?

Having the licence to be a completely self-indulgent luvvy for a bit is my reward for giving up five years of my spare time*.

I mean, people are actually paying money to see my work! Jesus effin Christ! Nobody, in the history of the world, has ever paid money to watch an advert.

I apologise. But sod it. I cannot assume this is ever going to happen to me again, so I HAVE to milk it for all it is worth.

The other night, I had the absolute pleasure of watching the film with a bunch of my old football teammates from Hyde Park Thursdays FC (Team catchphrases include... 'Forever purple', 'Put a purple head on it', 'Shin pads in the cup', 'Who's finishing stronger?' ...You had to be there.) It was great to see the boys again and talk about old times. Although, if anyone overheard us in the pub afterwards, they would have been forgiven for thinking we were former professional standard players rather than the South London Christian League parks footballers that we were.

Next night was the Agency Night At The Pictures. The agency bosses made a very nice gesture of buying a block of tickets to one of the public performances for people at work.

It was brilliant. Although, a little bit of a shame that a big new business pitch the following morning meant that a lot of my favourite people had to work late and, therefore, could not attend. But that's advertising for you**.

On the same night, the director's advertising production company put on a private screening for ad industry types in the screening room of the Charlotte Street Hotel. So I found myself behaving like a social butterfly and attending the pre-drinks of the production company screening, before hotfooting it to The Brixton Ritzy cinema to hook up with all my colleagues at the agency one. It was lovely to see some old mukkas at the private screening, along with the advertising liggers who turn up to anything involving free drinks.

There was even a former boss of mine who turned up. I thought this was particularly magnanimous of him seeing that, as far as I can remember, he didn't like me.

It would have been nice to stick around for the after-drinks,. But I couldn't not watch the film with my workmates, could I?

It was interesting doing so, because, out of all the audiences I've been in, this lot seemed to respond the most to all the little dark humoured moments we put in. There was more laughter, basically. It could be that they were expecting some dark humour, because they know me well, or it could simply have been the fact that it was a 9pm showing, and most of them were half cut by the time the curtains parted. Probably a bit of both, to be fair.

It was certainly a happily drunken night afterwards. Only slightly dampened by two crack-heads getting lairy with me in the queue of Brixton McDonalds at the end of the night.

Another night I watched the film with a diverse bunch of people that included some elderly relatives, a cousin, a childhood friend of my missus, my stepdaughter and some of her mates. Again, it was a really lovely night. And there were no crack-heads involved, either.

It's a special time, all right. What a lucky so and so I am.

Just cycling past the local cinema after a trying day at work and seeing the poster shining from the lightbox is such a buzz.

Tonight, as the cinematic run comes to its end***, there is one final film related experience to go through.

Picturehouse Cinemas want the producer, the director, a couple of the actors and myself to attend a Q&A screening.

Gulp.

A Q&A screening is where the audience watch the film and then get to ask the director/actors questions afterwards.

I have attended a few of these down the years, in the audience, but I've never been to one with a writer on stage. So I never imagined I would ever be required to be a sweating, blushing, emotional tit at the front, myself.

Shit. I only agreed to do it as moral support for the director. And guess what? Now it's come to it, he's cried off because it clashes with his blinking holiday.

So I find myself nervously downing more pints than is advisable in the Picturehouse bar with the producer and a couple of the actors on a Thursday night. The film is playing as we drink. And the idea is we go in for the Q&A at the end of the film.

The others all seem completely relaxed. They've done this sort of thing loads of times. Standing up (well, sitting down) in front of paying members of the public and being questioned about my work is something I've never ever done. Scary as hell.

I've spent the three weeks since I first heard I was doing this, inwardly rehearsing intelligent responses to the questions I imagine I might be asked.

Some of the critics have been a bit hung up on perceived sociological and gender issues in the story. I'm ready for a similar line of questioning tonight. I have to be careful, because it's probably very easy when defending yourself against sociological/gender accusations to come across as the exact thing your trying to defend yourself against.

Being a little tipsy might be good for the nerves, but it does nothing for the lucidity of one's arguments. But, yeah, I will have another pint, thank you very much.

After taking a photo of us all sticking our fingers up to send to our absent holidaying director, we finish our drinks and head inside the screening room.

Bloody hell. I sheepishly take my seat at the front beside my confident friends. I can barely muster the bottle to look up and acknowledge the audience sitting in front of me. Being a cinema, the seats bank up sharply in front of us, which makes it feel even more intimidating. Despite the air-con, I find myself sweating straight away.

However, we have a moderator - the programmes curator of Picturehouse cinemas - and he starts the proceedings with some simple friendly questions for us.

Our producer is in his element. He loves holding court, and with the spotlight literally on him he is really on one.

Then, the other actors weigh in with some interesting stuff about their involvement in the project.

Our male lead says how excited he was when he read the script. He was in LA for the pilot season out there when, ironically, a script from London arrived. It was like nothing else he had been offered, because it gave him the chance to play a character that is completely different to the juvenile comedy character that he is famous for in the UK. And that he filmed an impromptu audition tape on his phone that he sent to the director and I in order to get the role.

Our lovely second lead actress talks about how her friendship and previous working relationship with our BLA (brilliant leading actress) really helped them to convincingly play sisters with a complex sibling relationship in the film.

And, while mopping my brow, I try my best to explain the real-life incident that happened to the director several years ago that became the seed that sprouted the idea for the film.

With the Q&A successfully warmed up, the moderator does the thing I've been dreading and opens the questions to the room.

I brace myself for accusations.

They don't arrive.

All the audience want to do is ask the well-known actors stuff. Not the inarticulate fatty. Although, one question is thrown my way, which is: 'Are you working on any projects right now?'

My reply of 'Yes, a cooking sauce brand' is completely lost on everyone. So I quickly follow it up by saying that having an advertising background means I'm not locked into any sort of genre in particular. As an ad man, I am used to switching between different tones of voice, depending on the target audience of the brand I am working on****. I am, therefore, comfortable, happy even, to switch between genres on different projects. And the current screenplay I'm working on is a daft comedy, not a thriller.

As the producer talks for England some more, I realise that this Q&A thing isn't so bad after all. The audience are not there to grill the panel like it's BBC Question Time. They actually enjoyed the film and they are interested in what we've got to say.

I relax a bit. And spend the rest of the experience trying to do what I've tried to do during all the other experiences I've been lucky enough to have during this process. That is, do my best to completely enjoy them in the moment.

That is what this brilliant adventure has been about. Enrichment. Enriching experiences, anyway. Not financial enrichment particularly.

If I work out how much I've been paid for the amount of time I've put into this project, I reckon I'd have been better off, financially, if I'd worked in a bar. But it's not about money. Not at the moment, anyway.

Christ knows where it will all lead, though. It might lead absolutely nowhere, or it might open a door into a whole new career that doesn't involve arguing with marketers about how compelling or not television audiences find the ingredients of a chocolate bar.

As this project has shown, I can't rely on getting my own original material produced to make a living.

If I were to leap into a proper writing career, I'd need to get writing on existing TV series and films in development in a constant stream of rewrites. It would probably be a lot of hard work to make anywhere near the amount of money that I currently earn in advertising. And that's only if I'm good enough.

I read a magazine article about a hot TV writer recently. She said that one of the greatest thing about getting her second major TV series commissioned was that she could give up her waitressing job.

Gulp. I'd make a lousy waitress.

And anyway, could it ever be as effin fantastically brilliant when it's a job? When it's not an antidote to something that's a grind, will it end up feeling like a grind, itself?

There is a fair chance that being a full-time writer might not be a better option in reality than the copywriter/screenwriter gig I currently have.

Why be average at two careers? Maybe earning a decent living at one and keeping the other as a magical hobby is the best I can hope for.

But on the other hand, a world without any wrist-slitting conversations with marketers about chocolate bar ingredients and the like is my Xanadu.

Oh I dunno. I just dunno.

So even more reason to enjoy this last bit of film world magic tonight, I think.

When I step out into the balmy night air after the Q&A and hug and wave off the actors and producer departing in their paid-for chauffer-driven cars, I have no bitterness that muggins is the only one who has to get the train home.

I am just happy to have had yet another wonderful experience on this (hopefully more than) once-in-a-lifetime journey. I am a happy man.

Tonight is the last night of the general release.

But tonight, for me, is a lovely full stop.

There's a beautiful melancholia about watching the cinema staff take down our posters. I nab one and roll it up, ready to be framed and hung in my hallway as a daily reminder of the best eighteen months of my life.

As I sit on the last train home clutching my souvenir as carefully and proudly as I held the goldfish I won at the fair, aged seven, I reflect on all the wonderful things that have happened to me. The people I've met, the red carpets I've stepped on, the column inches that have been written. I never thought any of it would ever happen. But it did. The rewards for me have been manifold. I am far better at my day job thanks to my hobby. This has been a big lift to my general demeanor. Ask my missus.

Also, being able to call myself a copywriter/screenwriter gives me a point of difference to my peers.

I mean, Jesus, if it wasn't for the screenwriting, I probably would have had to grow a hipster beard and roll up my trousers to remain relevant in ad land.

Yes, not having to go for the 1970s kiddy fiddler look, like many other ad folk are these days, is a huge reward in itself.

At the risk of sounding like a shit motivational speaker, I want to say this: If there is something in life you want to achieve – a dream, or an ambition of any description – then fucking go for it. And don't let anyone or anything put you off. Not even your own low expectations or cynicism. Because stars do align. Unlikely things do happen.

Heck, even if those wondrous stars don't align, the act of backing yourself and having a right good go at it can only be a positive thing.

Tonight, I never thought I'd enjoy speaking in front of a paying audience at a Q&A. But I did enjoy it.

And I genuinely think that the audience did, too.

All seventeen of them.

FADE TO BLACK:

The End.

** You may well argue that by writing in excess of sixty-thousand words about oneself means I've been a self-indulgent luvvy for the last year and a half.*

*** I've also learned and accepted the fact that, just because something is really really important to you, does not mean it is at all important to others.*

Some people, who have been very interested and supportive throughout, did not, when it came to it, bother to watch the film.

It doesn't matter that it's the product of my entire heart and soul for five years of my life. For others, if the screening's on a Wednesday and that's the night they have to collect little Johnny from his Jujitsu class, they won't be at the screening.

Absolutely fine.

One bloke from work, however – an editor, who has come across as being really interested all the way through – actually took the trouble to come and tell me that he wasn't going to the agency film night, because it's in Brixton and he doesn't like going south of the river.

Err, thanks for letting me know. I could be really bitchy and say that it's this lack of positive energy that has made him only get as far in his career as being an ad agency mood film editor by the age of forty, but I'm not bitchy like that.

No, I have to accept that some people are generous spirited and others are not.

I'd like to think that I am a generous spirited person and would support anyone who had something important going on. But maybe it's the same as those times I haven't turned up for a colleague's leaving drinks when, even though I really like them, I'd been out the previous night and I didn't want to overdo it.

Of course, the more simple and plausible explanation for the absentees is they think I'm a complete tosser. So, on balance, I'm grateful to those who did turn up.

**** It was only supposed to run for one week, but it got an extra week due to popular demand. Get in!*

***** In a normal week I could be simultaneously advertising to jaded commuters for a train company, mums about cooking sauce, left-leaning conscientious folk on behalf of a charity, and fat comfort-eating middle-aged women for bloody chocolate bars.*

PART SIX

POST-RELEASE

Sorry, I thought I'd put this thing to bed.

I didn't realise the gift would keep on giving like it has. I'm talking film festivals, baby.

DINARD

I'M ON A WEEK OFF from work and I'm being flown to France for an all-expenses trip to a film festival.

I am one of three representatives of my movie that meet at London City Airport to board a chartered BA plane to Dinard in Brittany, France.

I have told everyone at work that it is a private jet. Obviously, it's not a Lear jet with a Jacuzzi and strippers, as I've painted it to them. But it is privately chartered and there are no propellers. So, technically, that's a private jet, yes?

I love City Airport. For one, it costs £1.50 to get there on the DLR and takes twenty minutes from my home, door-to-door. The other thing is, it's tiny, so it takes next to no time at all to get through security etc. Therefore, I don't feel at all like punching a defenceless small animal by the time I meet my travelling companions on this tres jolie jolly in the departure lounge. They are the producer, and the excellent leading male actor. We are all excited to be here. After coffee and croissants (when on your way your to Rome and all that), we board the flight. There is a smattering of well-known faces from the film world aboard. (One of them is our male leading actor.) The rest of the plane is filled with film world people, too.

We checked in separately, so have been allocated seats apart. This suits me fine. It's an hour's hop to Dinard, which I use to write a page of my new screenplay.

Before I know it, I'm switching off my laptop and buckling my seatbelt for landing. I breeze through airport immigration like a hot knife through unsalted butter. (We're in France now.) And reconnect with the guys at baggage reclaim. I don't have a bag to reclaim, and I'm busting for a slash, so we agree to meet up outside.

I am the first one from the flight to walk out of the arrivals gate. Bizarrely, along with the usual smattering of world-weary middle-aged men holding white boards with people's names inked on them, there is a bank of photographers and film crews. As the automatic doors swish open, they collectively head turn to me, expectantly. $1/10^{th}$ of a second later they collectively go back to what they were doing.

I laugh to myself. I take a quick pish. I go out and stand among the cab drivers (sans board blanc) and watch while the other, more illustrious members of our flight emerge to flash bulbs, excitement and microphones shoved in faces.

We reconnect as a trio and are directed to one of two coaches that have been chartered to transfer us to our hotels. The last time I had a flight with a coach hotel transfer attached to it, I was twenty and it was Faliraki. Decades later, I play the same game of judging all the hotels we stop off at en-route and speculating whether ours will be better/worse. Ours is better than most. Pretty good. Despite being 1970/80s build with original decor, it actually works in a slightly kitsch timepiece kind of way. Three stars. And the view from my balcony across the sandy bay is *formidable.* Oh, and it's free.

We meet back in the lobby after a quick ten-minute hotel room orientation. The first thing we need to do is collect our festival passes from the Grand Palais de Film. These are important things to have, as they will gain us free entry to as many films as we like for the duration of the festival. I could see the building from my balcony over the other side of the pretty sandy horseshoe bay. So rather than take the road, I suggest we stroll through the hotel gardens and along the promenade to the festival building.

It is most agreeable taking in the sea air, the Gallic gull screams and the warmth of the French Indian summer sun as we walk. It's lovely. People are sitting at pavement cafés eating moules. There are locals playing boules on the beach. It couldn't be more typically French if a geezer in a beret wandered over and tried to flog us some onions.

We arrive at the Grand Palais. The grand entrance is at the top of the cliff, but this is the beach entrance. It doesn't feel quite right, but we head in anyway. We encounter a festival employee. She seems surprised to see us. Her English is not great. But between our schoolboy French and her ecole Anglais, we realise this is the tradesman's entrance.

She leads us through the bowels of the building and takes us up in the service lift, on the way stopping to let in a tradesman with a job lot of self-standing placard posts (posts to put placards on). It's not every day you see a famous bloke off the telly politely lugging placard posts into a service elevator, is it?

We make it to the lobby and collect our accreditation. It comes with a festival brochure, and invitations to some exclusive screenings and cocktail parties, all packaged in a little canvas laptop bag. It's a pretty naff item, is the laptop bag. But everyone at work will absolutely hate it when I skip into the office next week swinging it gleefully.

After a quick look at the festival timetable, we decide we need to luncheon now. We've got films to watch!

We'd like to go back to the beach where there are cafes serving moules. But we can't work out how to get back there without impromptu manual labour being involved, so we search for somewhere at road level, instead. We quickly find several. But they are mostly shut. It's past three o'clock in the afternoon and we're in France.

The fifth place we try is open. We grab a table dans le terrace and immediately order a bottle of rouge. Priorities sorted, we ask the waiter for the menu as he pours our glasses. He sheepishly points to a tiny section of the drinks menu. Either the kitchen proper is shut in the afternoon, or this is just a bar. Not a bistro. Fuck-sticks. The blimmin' wine's poured now. We have no alternative but to order from this shite bar menu.

I'm in the gastronomic capital of the world and I'm eating the gastronomic equivalent of a British Rail sandwich circa 1981. The producer has chosen slightly better than the actor and I, with a cheese toasty, but sacrebleu!

We get it over with as quickly as possible and then head for the cinema to watch our first film of the festival. There are six cinemas dotted around the town of Dinard that are showing festival films. We follow the map to find the correct cinema, but it seems our geography is as keen as our nose for restaurants, because we end up walking half way around the town before finally finding the place and realising it is literally around the corner from our shit lunch spot.

Still, being able to walk past a huge queue of the public and flashing our passes to gain entry, puts me in a better mood.

Hanging out with a famous person is interesting. They are magnets for attention, of course. But it seems they are also magnets for other famous people. We get inside, take our seats and immediately another famous bloke - a well-known actor and director - comes over and sits with us. Nice bloke. A laugh.

The film is really good. It's called '71. I recommend it.

As the rest of the audience leave at the end, we hang about. For in twenty minutes our film is on in the same cinema.

We grab a quick beer. We head back inside and are introduced onto the stage by a French compere. There are about two hundred and fifty in the audience. The actor and I stand there like idiots as the producer says a few words in his best pidgin French. He loves public speaking in any language. He thinks he's managed to get a laugh until he realises that the writer standing next to him is taking a photo of the audience and waving at them.

We say our merci beaucoups and get off the stage. We are due at the official festival opening ceremony in an hour, so the other two head straight back to the hotel to get showered and changed. Seeing as I have no smarter clothes to change into, I decide to hang about and watch some of the film, instead. It is really lovely and really weird to watch it with subtitles. It is definitely another addition to my highlights reel of experiences.

After staying until the end of act one, I reluctantly bail. It's too late to meet the guys back at the hotel, so I head straight for the Palais. As I arrive, a phalanx (I love that word) of photographers starts snapping away. Their flashguns combine to create a strobe light effect. They are not trained on me, of course. It's for the arrival of Catherine Denueuve, the chairman of the judges.

I head inside and find the cocktail party and my mates. We get talking to a famous director whose film is opening the festival. This is a big deal. But he is nervous about the few words he has to get up and say to everyone beforehand. We reassure him that it will be great and promise to hook up for drinks later on.

We leave the director to mingle, and head to the cinema screen to grab decent seats for the grand opening ceremony. It's a bit of a hike from the cocktail lounge and we're feeling a bit gutted for the director, and the festival as a whole, when we take our seats. The room is only half full. I mean, bloody hell. Think of all the time and expense that has gone into holding this event. People have been flown in! The least they could do is bother their arses to turn up to the- Oh, hold on...

Light fills the screen and the half-full auditorium is explained. On screen is an image of another, much bigger auditorium, which is packed to the rafters with people and Catherine Deneuve giving a speech on stage. That is Le Grand Palais Auditorium. We are in the Le Petits Palais (it's still a two hundred and fifty seat theatre).

We are the overspill!

A ripple of laughter reverberates around the room as everyone realises that we are the film festival equivalent of being on the kid's table. But we still have to endure forty-five minutes of watching the grown-ups make a succession of speeches in English that are translated on stage into French. It's like Eurovision without the music. By the time our director friend has said his witty and eloquent few words, we're an hour behind schedule. (Ha! One drink with the guy and I'm calling him my friend.) The producer wonders out loud whether we should forget the film and go and have dinner somewhere. I've only had a British Rail sandwich and a croissant all day. It sounds like a bloody good idea. No one will know. We're in the overspill. But the actor is adamant that we should watch the film. He's right. Knowing our luck, we'll sneak out of the theatre and bump straight into the only other person who won't be staying to watch the film - our director friend.

We knuckle down and sit through the film like good children. But as the credits roll we bolt from the venue like nine-year-olds who've just heard the peel of an ice cream van on the street.

Again, the first place we find turns out to be a bar, not a restaurant. We're not making that mistake again. We make to leave, but are stopped by a big French dude. Luckily, he doesn't want to start any trouble, but to congratulate us. It turns out he was at the screening earlier and really enjoyed the film. Wow.

We end up in a pizza joint (I know, not French. But, fuck it, je suis tres Hank Marvin). I reflect on what just happened in the bar. The actor smiles a knowing smile. I realise that I have just had a glimpse into his world of being stopped by strangers who say nice things to you. It's surreal. It's not getting hassled and stared at all the time, like he, no doubt, has to deal with. It's just someone being nice.

This, and the huge calzone now in my stomach give me such a warm glowing feeling that I don't mind when the other fellas wimp out of carrying on the piss after dinner.

Over the next twenty-four hours, several more people approach us and say how much they liked the film. (On one occasion, it was in a darkened cinema. How the hell did she recognise us?)

I have plans for the weekend that I can't cancel, so I can't stay for the rest of the festival. I miss our big screening in the Grand Palais. Although the overspill cinema wasn't required, the guys say the film played out well to in excess of four hundred people.

I also don't get to fly back on the charter jet. Nevertheless, as I bite into my €6 sandwich on a cramped Ryanair aircraft - the aeronautical equivalent of a chicken sandwich in a shitty Brittany wine bar - I am flying, literally and figuratively.

SHANGHAI SURPRISE

I AM DRAGGING MY WHEELIE bloody suitcase along the uneven pavements of Southwark, all a fluster. I need to get to the offices of the visa service I have naively appointed to handle my Chinese visa application. And I need to get there bloody fast.

This is the first leg of a protracted journey to The 18th Shanghai International Film Festival that the director and I are quietly thrilled to have been asked to attend as representatives of our film.

However, I'm going nowhere without a passport. Despite getting on the case with the visa people over a week ago and selecting a service that was supposed to cost £75 and take 4 days, it's now 4 hours before my flight to Shanghai departs and they have only just managed to get my passport stamped.

Apparently, the Chinese authorities are suspicious of people with the job title 'writer'. It took three applications before they would issue me with one. I imagine by the third application, someone at the embassy looked me up and realised that the twaddle I write is a zero threat to the People's Republic.

Jesus. I'm only going for three days. What a palaver. It's been a stressful process. Particularly when considering that I paid someone to take the stress away.

I'm so relieved to finally pick up my passport, that on the tube to Heathrow I decide not to blow a fuse when I read the invoice and see that the application fee came in at over £250 in the end.

When I meet the director in the Virgin lounge, the bonhomie of cramming as many free cocktails down our necks in 40 minutes as possible, means we shrug our shoulders to the notion that the visa service probably invented most of the drama of the past week in order to push up their fee.

The flight is pretty uneventful. I had planned to spend the time working on my latest screenplay. But the combination of cocktails and visa stress means I spend the eleven hours watching movies rather than writing one. (Plus about 20-40 minutes of sleep, tops.)

When we walk out of the arrivals gate at Pudong Airport and see that none of the hundreds of boards being held up have our names scribbled on them, we realise that this isn't like an advertising trip.

We lament that we normally have a producer with us to sort the transportation, check in to the hotels, book the restaurants, show us the sights etc.

Fuck it, we're big boys. We decide to get the tube to the hotel.

45 minutes later, we have finally worked out where we need to go on the metro map and bought the correct tickets in the machine (They cost about 70p each). We're proud of ourselves as we board the train.

Shit the actual bed, Shanghai is big. Even if it wasn't for the thirteen hours of travelling that preceded it, this tube journey feels like an eternity. I mean, London is big, but this place is something else. The population is in excess of 25 million. (London is about 8 million.) I am awed and disconcerted in equal measure.

Then add the mile walk from the metro station to the hotel, dragging our suitcases across Southwark-esque pavements in 30° heat. It means that by the time I get to my room (21st floor, amazing views of this megalopolis) all I want to do is crash out.

But I can't.

We've got the opening ceremony of the festival tonight. I've got to keep going or I will keel over.

So I have a quick shower, then head back down to the lobby to meet the director. We jump in a cab and head for Shanghai's version of the British Film Institute to register in the festival.

We get our plastic ID and a bag full of literature then find somewhere to eat. Turns out it's an Italian restaurant. We're after authentic Chinese. So we have a beer and head back to the hotel. There are three restaurants in the hotel. They are all shut. No problem. The bar serves food. We order 'Shanghai Noodles' twice and a beer each.

We're hopeful. It seems like a classy bar. So classy, in fact, that the little vases on each table have tiny goldfish swimming in them. Seriously.

Our food arrives. Blimey, we've spent our whole lives tasting bad Chinese food in Britain, but it's taken us to fly half way around the world to China itself to actually get the nastiest Chinese food we've ever bloody tasted.

A couple of chopstick-fulls are all we can muster. And anyway, the coach has turned up to ferry all of us international delegates to the opening ceremony. The invitation says 'formal dress'. The best we can do is t-shirts with collars. All the other delegates from around the world have read the script, however, and are turned out in their finest eveningwear.

As we near the venue, we realise just how inappropriately we are dressed. The venue is the Chinese equivalent of the Royal Festival Hall. There is a Police cordon 150 yards around the theatre to keep the crowds back. We have to go through three lots of security to get to the theatre. The event is being broadcast live on national Chinese TV to a billion people. And we look like we are there to fix the air conditioning.

We stroll in, a little bewildered and watch the photographers and TV crews surrounding lots of beautiful Chinese people on the red carpet. Given the glamour and excitement, we deduce that they are Chinese movie stars.

Talk about surreal. We take a few photos of the Chinese celebrities, almost out of politeness. Then we try and find something to eat.

Shit. There are no refreshments on offer, whatsoever. There is still over an hour to go until the ceremony starts. So we go through the three lots of security in reverse and try and find somewhere to eat.

We find a little dumpling place in a back street. This is EXACTLY what we have been after all day. The menu is four dishes. We point at the most appetising photograph on the wall. The dumplings are made to order and arrive in a chilli broth. It's lovely, hearty stuff, which, with a soft drink, costs us 12 Yuan, each (£1.20).

We head back to the glitzy ceremony. We're accosted by ticket touts who offer us $100 each for our tickets.

We finally take our seats in the glitzy auditorium and watch the opening ceremony.

What was it like? Well, imagine attending a glamorous high-profile event like the BAFTAs, but not recognising a single person, or understanding a single word of the proceedings. You haven't slept for thirty-six hours and you're wearing jeans, t-shirt and trainers. Yeah, It was a bit odd.

But it gets odderer.

After the event, a fleet of buses appear to whisk all attendees from the Chinese equivalent of the Royal Festival Hall to the after party at the Chinese equivalent of Excel exhibition centre.

It sounds shit, but we go along with it, anyway. It takes forever to get there. But despite being at Excel, it is an ultra chic party, full to the absolute brim with the beautiful people of Shanghai. There are photographers and TV cameras abound. There is even a drone floating about on the terrace filming us. It is as glamorous a do as any exclusive film industry party in any city in the world. The only thing they seem to have got wrong is the music, which is akin to a disco in a working men's club. That, and letting some air conditioning engineers in, of course.

Christ knows what they thought of us two planks propping up the bar in scruffy gear, inhaling the Champagne and vol au vents. Maybe they think we're famous western filmmakers, or something, because no one's looking down at us, like people would at the London or Hollywood equivalent of this party. We even get talking to a few people.

I've never felt such a surreal, sleep deprived intoxication as this. I am an alien landed in a strange land. Just walking around the streets is strange enough, but the added surrealism of being dropped into these elitist situations is too much. What with the limitless free Champagne on offer and all.

We end up back at the hotel bar at 2am drinking beer and talking shit with a Lithuanian film producer that we shared a cab home with from the after party.

When I finally call a night on what I estimate to be a 33-hour day, I get my final Shanghai surprise of the evening. The bog has an in-built bidet thing in the seat. Let me tell you, it is quite a shock when you're as drunk and jet-lagged as I am.

Next morning, I meet the director in the breakfast room, bright and early. We pick at the ropey hotel breakfast before heading out. We have Wi-Fi in our rooms, but have found that we can't log onto many of the western websites. A reminder that even though we're in the biggest city in the world, as hi-tech and international as any other, it's in a country with a lot of restrictions. Facebook and Twitter are down, so I can't brag about the trip to people at home. And Google doesn't work, so it's quite hard to get any tourist information about Shanghai. All we have is a paper map and a vague idea of where to go.

We get a cab to Nanking Road. This is the biggest shopping street in the whole of China. It's quite a sight. It contains every single western brand and retail outlet you can imagine, but not many Chinese brands. It's funny being here and seeing all these American, British and European brands being consumed voraciously by the Chinese. It sums up the new China to me. Because it is all about status and being seen to embrace western culture. The Chinese love brands. Even though 98% of these brands are actually made in China for tuppence, the people of Shanghai are happy to pay top dollar for them if they have the right western logo on them. Neither of us is into shopping, but the one shop we walk into is Nike Town. Amazingly, the shoes in there - all made in China, of course - are actually more expensive here than in London. We paid £1.20 for a meal, remember, so if you can afford to wear £120 Nike trainers in China, you must be pretty wealthy.

The other thing that strikes me in this concrete megalopolis is the complete lack of graffiti and bicycles. China couldn't be more synonymous with bicycles. But that's the old China. The China of Beijing, communism and great walls. Shanghai is the new China. I literally see two people on bikes the whole time I'm here. And they are both Lycra-clad westerners on road bikes. Shanghai is the city of cars and highways. The two-wheeled transportation of choice is the electric moped. Brilliant! Why don't we have them in London? The only problem is that they are pretty silent and people ride them here on pavements and through red lights. So you have to keep your wits about you. The director and I are both relieved to be fully paid up members of the Tufty Club right now. Particularly as neither of us thought of getting travel insurance sorted for this trip.

At the end of Nanking Road is The Bund, the most famous riverside strip in China. The Bund is where old Shanghai meets modern Shanghai. And is the place where every postcard view of the city is taken from.

Apparently, the done thing is to have lunch at one of the rooftop restaurants while admiring the breath-taking skyline across the river. Even though it's not even midday yet, it's so swelteringly hot and our body clocks are so all over the place, we go for it.

The place we find is a European bistro-style kind of restaurant. We sit on the terrace. It's beautiful. It's one of those places that make you feel happy and privileged to be there. For somewhere so well to do, the food isn't fantastic. But they have an interesting alcohol deal of drink-as-much-rose-wine-as-you-like-in-two-hours-for-220Yuan (£22).

Three hours later we're on bloody good form as we stumble out of there. The kindly waitress has written down a list of good places to hang out. So we fall into a cab, point at one of the names on the list and are driven to the Shanghai equivalent of Covent Garden. We stroll around for a bit, before finding a pavement bar to get stuck in to the beers.

We are both as funny as fuck and the world is all put right. Then one of us remembers that we have the Q&A screening of our film this evening. It is basically, the whole reason for us being in Shanghai. Shit, we need to get back to the hotel, get changed, meet our chaperone and drive to the cinema. I'd better drink up.

Hang on, there's a cinema on the other side of the square. I have a look. It's only the blinking cinema where our blinking Q&A screening is being held!

Cheers! We'll drink to that wonderful piece of serendipity.

So that's why, four hours later, the director and I stand in t-shirts and shorts with sunburnt foreheads before an audience of over three hundred people.

We're well chuffed with the size of the audience. But I suppose one thing Shanghai is not short of is people.

We are handed ceremonial buckets of popcorn and microphones. A dandy host talks to the audience in Chinese. There's a round of applause. Then he turns to us and speaks in

Chinese. An interpreter then whispers the questions to us in English and relays our answers back to the audience in Chinese.

Despite this stiltedness, it goes pretty well. The questions are a lot about the main character in the film being a single career woman, which, I suppose, is not probably as common here as it is in the west.

They seem pretty interested. However, by far the biggest reaction we get is when I say that, yes, we love Shanghai and we'd love to make a movie over here.

Unfortunately, they don't open the questions up to the audience, which is a shame. It's all wrapped up in about 25 minutes. We get a big round of applause, are handed big bunches of flowers and stand for loads of photographs with various people. They must think we're famous or something, because we're getting a lot of attention. And who are we to put them straight?

The dandy host then introduces us to some actors and actresses and we are invited to join them at a party in another part of the city.

Ten minutes later we are tooling across Shanghai in the back of a BMW with smirks on our faces. One of the actresses is really interested in what I think about Shanghai and China. I say that everyone likes China and that there being China towns in cities all over the world proves its popularity. She is disappointed with my answer, though.

"But that's old China" she says. Blimey, they really want to be seen as a modern sophisticated city.

We get to the party. It's on another rooftop on The Bund overlooking the stunning skyline. At night it looks like a scene from Blade Runner. The sides of the buildings have actually been turned into giant LED billboards. It's really impressive.

But the party isn't. It's actually finishing. Our hosts are a bit embarrassed. We have a drink, anyway. We are introduced to a bloke who is described as a huge producer and distributer in the Chinese film industry. The director swaps business cards with him and we get our picture taken together. But the party is so fizzled out now we have no choice but to leave. There are about a dozen of us standing on a street corner. Maybe our new friends have worked out that we aren't famous and interesting after all, because one of them suddenly announces that they have another party to go to, but we can go to a bar down the street with two of the actresses. One of the appointed girls immediately declares that she is going to the other party, too. But the other girl is really happy to hang with us. And she keeps asking if we can cast her in our next film. I suddenly feel really uncomfortable. This is not right. What the fuck? I start thinking of how we can go for one drink and then make our excuses and leave, but the director is more strident. He hails a cab and we put her in it.

Bloody hell. That spoiled the night that did. Suddenly feeling really cheap, we hail another cab and point to another of the names in the list of places to go.

We are driven to a high-end hotel somewhere. The cab driver has already conned us by saying the fare is 100Yuan. (£10. It should be about 40Yuan.) But on arrival he chances his arm further by saying he meant 100Yuan each. We laugh in his face and tell him to fuck right off, which he understands despite knowing no English.

The hotel bar is dead. We have one and leave. We're bloody hungry. We decide to go for a wander and find a local place to eat. It's late and everywhere is shut. We end up hopelessly lost, in a not very shiny part of the city, eating in a local noodle place that's about to close for the night.

As the director and I sit and eat our surprisingly fantastic late night food, we reflect on the absolutely mental events of the previous couple of days. And also the amazing journey that we've been on together. It began with us sitting in a similarly grotty restaurant in Soho about ten years ago imagining how great it would be to make a feature film.

And it has been great. We've literally come a long way.

"I'll get this, mate." I say when the 20Yuan (£2) bill arrives. It's the least I could do. Especially after he paid 400Yuan (£40) for two beers in the hotel bar earlier.

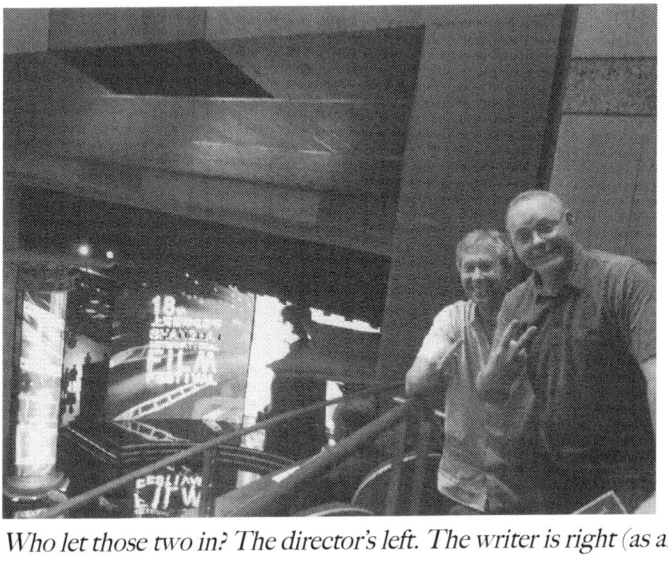

Who let those two in? The director's left. The writer is right (as always).

EPILOGUE

KEEPING ROSY, starring Maxine Peake, Blake Harrison and Christine Bottomley, enjoyed a nationwide cinematic release in summer 2014, through Picturehouse Cinemas. And a month-long 'immersive cinema experience' release in a pop-up cinema venue in Manchester.

The film had a gala screening at the Raindance London Film Festival in October 2014, and was part of the Official Selection at the Dinard festival, France.

In December 2014, Keeping Rosy was nominated for a prestigious Moet British Independent Film Award.

The awards ceremony was held at the Old Billingsgate Market, a venue that the author had previously attended for ad awards.

The night was exactly the same as an advertising awards do. Except for the three hundred excited film fans at the entrance, the red carpet area with the phalanx of paparazzi photographers and the dozens of world-renowned film stars present.

When he read all about the night in the next morning's newspapers, hung over like a dog, the author realised it was the first awards ceremony he'd attended that was of interest to anyone other than just the people getting drunk at the ceremony.

In 2015, Keeping Rosy was part of the Official Selection of the Bordeaux film festival, The 18th Shanghai International Film Festival, and the Porto Film Festival, where Maxine Peake won the Best Actress award for her lead performance. KR was also awarded the Best Film Award at the Isle of Wight Film Festival.

The film was broadcast on Sky and BBC television in 2015 and 2016, respectively. And is available on demand through iTunes, Amazon and Blinkbox.

The DVD is available at Amazon.co.uk and would make a wonderful purchase for yourself or a loved one.

The chocolate bar commercial cost two-thirds of the price of the feature film to make, but never aired.

The author is still a full-time ad man, part-time screenwriter. He currently has five feature-film projects in various stages of development.

Oh, and he's just finished his first book. As have you.

ACKNOWLEDGEMENTS

I'D LIKE TO THANK EVERYONE who has played a part in making the last couple of years so memorable, whether they have been directly referenced in this rambling account, or not. I'm talking about my family, my friends and my colleagues. There are, of course, several people whom I owe a particular debt of gratitude...

Steve, Isabelle, Richard, Maxine, Chrissy and Blake for your wonderful talent, friendship and generosity.

Lee for suggesting I write it all down. Nice one, Onkle.

Gaz for the cover design. I'm with you all the way, brother.

Mum for the diligent proof reading, and giving birth to me.

I hope I haven't got anything wrong. And apologies for the sweariness. My only intention was to jot stuff down as I saw it, and try and make it a bit of a laugh.

23009318R00202

Printed in Great Britain
by Amazon